HISTORIES OF A RADICAL BOOK

HISTORIES OF A RADICAL BOOK

E. P. Thompson and *The Making of the English Working Class*

Edited by

Antoinette Burton and Stephanie Fortado

berghahn
NEW YORK • OXFORD
www.berghahnbooks.com

Published in 2021 by
Berghahn Books
www.berghahnbooks.com

Originally published as a special issue of
Historical Reflections/Reflexions Historiques Volume 41, issue 1 (2015).

Library of Congress Cataloging-in-Publication Data

Names: Burton, Antoinette, 1961– editor. | Fortado, Stephanie, editor.
Title: Histories of a radical book : E. P. Thompson and the making of the English working class / edited by Antoinette Burton and Stephanie Fortado.
Other titles: Making of the English working class
Description: 1st Edition. | Brooklyn : Berghahn Books, 2020. | Includes bibliographical references and index.
Identifiers: LCCN 2020037118 | ISBN 9781789203288 (hardback) | ISBN 9781789204704 (paperback) | ISBN 9781789204728 (ebook)
Subjects: LCSH: Thompson, E. P. (Edward Palmer), 1924–1993—Political and social views. | Working class—England—History. | England—Social conditions.
Classification: LCC HD8388 .H57 2020 | DDC 305.5/620942—dc23
LC record available at https://lccn.loc.gov/2020037118

British Library Cataloguing in Publication Data

A catalogue record for this book is available from the British Library

ISBN 978-1-78920-328-8 hardback
ISBN 978-1-78920-470-4 paperback
ISBN 978-1-78920-472-8 ebook

Contents

Preface

The Revolution and the Book

Antoinette Burton and Stephanie Fortado

Does a revolution need big books anymore? Did it ever? As we write the preface to this re-publication of our retrospective special issue on E. P. Thompson's *The Making of the English Working Class* in the summer of 2020, it may not be the most important question. The people in the streets—Black, Brown, white—are raising fists and holding masks in place, not brandishing copies of books, whether larger or small. Some are turning, or returning, to James Baldwin. Others reach for Frantz Fanon. His recurrent arguments about the ways that colonial occupation made it "impossible … to breathe" are an uncanny reminder of the way it has always been for people oppressed because of the color of their skin.[1] Or, we read poetry—which, to recast Irish poet Eavan Boland, is "at once an archive of defeat and a diagram of victory."[2] In its comparatively small frame the poem holds the world, and seems well-suited to our TLDR/too long didn't read world. It's the perfect primer, readable off a small screen and committed easily to memory. Who has the time or patience to read big books now?

But if the answer is no one, what then are we to do with admonition of that great Irish-American labor leader "Mother" Mary Harris Jones, who nearly a century ago told West Virginia miners, "Get you some books and go into the shade while you are striking. Sit down and read. Educate yourself for the coming struggle."[3] And how do we account for the persistent links between protest and books? Think of the strike camps in late Victorian Australia, set up during the Shearers' Strike of 1891 to cater to the needs of strikers in Queensland. They had camp libraries aided by the *Worker* newspaper's free book exchange.[4] Or, think of the 1960s and 1970s book stores that served as vital gathering spaces for Black Power activists in the United States and as "pan-African sites of resistance" for Black British organizers.[5] Not to mention Occupy Wall Street, where one observer testified that "the uniting thread of dissatisfaction has given birth to a fresh emphasis on the right to knowledge, and the first institution of the people has been given form; The People's Library."[6]

Reading can and does give rise to direct action. In 2010 a small group of Chicago teachers, pleasing the ghost of Mother Jones and strikers before and after, formed a reading group where they pursued articles about the "corporate education reformers' attacks on public education and teachers" and Naomi Klein's *The Shock Doctrine,* in order to make sense of the undermining of public education they were experiencing in their city. That group of teachers would go on to take over the leadership of their union and lead a 2012 strike of third largest school district in the United States, helping to touch off a wave of teachers strikes that has since seen tens of thousands of educators walk of the job from Los Angeles to West Virginia, in the most sweeping labor actions to occur in the United States in decades.[7] If reading together still has a roll to play in waking the mostly slumbering body of U.S. labor, should Thompson's book make the reading list?

Especially as we consider the shifting landscape of class formations, where does a book about the working class fit? After a brief decline due to the Covid-19 pandemic and fluctuating stock markets, in less than one month after the stay-at-home order was issued in the United States, the total wealth of America's billionaires grew by $282 million, or nearly 10 percent. This after the U.S. billionaire wealth had already surged 1,130 percent between 1990 and 2020.[8] This trend is global, and in 2020 the United Nations World Social Report explained:

> Income inequality has increased in most developed countries and in some middle-income countries, including China and India, since 1990. Countries where inequality has grown are home to more than two thirds (71 percent) of the world population. [9]

As the chasms of wealth inequality widen and deepen across the globe, the very concept of the working class seems to rest on very shaky ground. This ground becomes shakier still when we consider what Ta-Nehisi Coates reminded in one of his much-read pieces in *The Atlantic,* "neighborhood poverty threatens both black poor and nonpoor families to such an extent *that poor white families are less likely to live in poor neighborhoods than nonpoor black families.*"[10] It would seem that any discussion of class that does not also talk about race has little to offer.

The Making of the English Working Class was never optimum on that score. The book is thin on the politics of race, except insofar as it is a monument to the presumptive whiteness of an artisanal-industrial revolution story shorn of its imperial bracings and apparently disconnected from the workings of global racial capital. In 1987 his rejoinder to Thompson, *The Making of the Black Working Class in Britain,* Ron Ramdin concludes his equally big book by recalling that

> According to E. P. Thompson, the English working class 'made itself as much as it was made.' He adds crucially … [that] 'class consciousness is the way in which experiences are handled in cultural terms: embodied in traditions, value-systems, ideas and institutional forms. If the experience appears as determined, class consciousness does not … class is defined by men as they live their own history, and, in the end, this is its only definition.'

"Indeed," Ramdin observed, "an integral part of these 'cultural terms' was racialism," which in turn "received the general endorsement of the white working class."[11]

Ramdin's book was published six years after riots by black youth broke out across the south of England, prompted by a series of racist murders ("Cartoon" Campbell and Akhtar Ali Baig among the victims) and the deaths of 13 young West Indian men in what has come to be called the New Cross Massacre, which "activated black consciousness into top gear." On March 2 1981 there was a day of action; 10,000 people marched through London "in a public display of black solidarity." Marchers and protesters were antagonized by police and baited by fascists; Brixton was on fire; property was damaged and "outside agitators" were blamed. April, May, June, July—marches and protests and "riots" continued. By midsummer, white youths had joined the protests in Liverpool and over two dozen other British cities, giving lie to headlines about "Black hot-heads" and proving, Ramdin reports, that police violence was the heart of the problem. *The Making of the Black Working Class in Britain* ends with the realistic but unhopeful conviction that "the disadvantages are too glaring to legitimize mere reforms."[12]

Or, perhaps, to legitimize mere books on the subject. To return to the themes of the original special issue, if Thompson's book is an artifact, dissatisfactions with the histories it told as well as with those it left out have led, directly and indirectly, to new histories of racial violence and to new forms of chronicling—and to new formats for reading them as well. For better or worse, you can get both Thompson's and Ramdin's tomes on Kindle. Meanwhile, the social media landscape of #BlackLivesMatter 2020 is bursting with reading lists. The earliest examples of this anti-racist genre were curated by two African American women librarians, Charlemae Rollins in Chicago and Augusta Baker in New York, in the 1940s as part of their wider anti-racist activism.[13] Rollins, granddaughter of enslaved people and a herself storyteller par excellence, called her 1948 reading list *We Build Together*; it featured children's books that boosted black children's self-esteem as well as guides for evaluating how well such books depicted black life.[14] Rollins and Baker—who contributed to *We Build Together* and also published her own list—were part of a larger community of dissident Black readers and librarians who saw the links between reading and anti-racist politics, and strove to get and keep books into activists' hands.[15]

Twenty years later, the 3rd edition of Rollins' book was issued by the National Council of Teachers of English, with place of publication listed as Champaign, Illinois—where our original Thompson retrospective conference was held and where this month young, high-fisted, peaceful Black Lives Matter protesters have filled the streets in the wake of the murder of George Floyd and those before and after. At this writing, the website of the local Champaign-Urbana Chapter of BLM advertises both a book drive and a long reading list, including a raft of children's literature titles by and about people of color.[16] These connections between youth reading and youth activism have globally Black antecedents, as Kasonde Thomas Mukonde's recent research on high school students' resistant reading in the Soweto of the 1960s and 1970s shows us.[17] Big or not, books (and books about books) may still be capable of illuminating geographies of solidarity, whether you read them before, during or after the revolution.

Antoinette Burton and Stephanie Fortado
Champaign-Urbana, IL
June 2020

Antoinette Burton *is Professor of History and Swanlund Endowed Chair at the University of Illinois, Urbana-Champaign, where she directs the Humanities Research Institute. Her most recent publication is a collection, co-edited with Renisa Mawani, called* Animalia: An Anti-Imperial Bestiary for Our Times *(2020).*

Stephanie Fortado *is a Lecturer at the Labor Education Program at the University of Illinois, Urbana Champaign, where she also co-directs the Regina V. Polk Women's Labor Leadership Conference. Her research focuses on labor, race and urban history, and she is currently completing a manuscript on how the Civil Rights and Black Power Movements shaped the public landscape in Cleveland, Ohio.*

Notes

1. Frantz Fanon, *Black Skin, White Masks* (NY: Grove Press, 1967), p. 226. We are grateful to Lou Turner for reminding us of the exact statement often misquoted ("It is not because the Indo-Chinese has discovered a culture of his own that he is in revolt. It is because 'quite simply' it was, in more than one way, becoming impossible for him to breathe") and of what Turner calls the "dialectic of breathing" across Fanon's body of work. For example, "There is not occupation of territory, on the one hand, and independence of persons on the other. It is the country as a whole, its history, its daily pulsation that are contested, disfigured, in the hope of a final destruction. Under these conditions, the individual's breathing is an observed, an occupied breathing. It is a combat breathing." ["Algeria Unveiled" (Appendix), in *Dying Colonialism*, 1967: 64-65].
2. Eavan Boland, *Object Lessons: The Life of the Woman and the Poet in Our Time* (W.W. Norton, 1995), p. 129.
3. Dale Fetherling, *Mother Jones the Miner's Angel* (Carbondale: Southern Illinois University Press, 1974), p. 91.
4. Among their most popular reads? Edward Bellamy's *Looking Backward* and Marx's *On Value*. See Stuart Svensen, *The Shearers' War: The Story of the 1891 Shearers' Strike* (U of Queensland Press, 1989), p. 117.
5. Joshua Clarke Davis, "Liberation Through Literacy: African American Bookstores, Black Power, and the Mainstreaming of Black Books," in *From Head Shops to Whole Foods: The Rise and Fall of Activist Entrepreneurs* (New York: Columbia University Press, 2017), 35-82; Colin A. Beckles, ""We Shall Not Be Terrorized Out of Existence": The Political Legacy of England's Black Bookshops." *Journal of Black Studies* 29, no. 1 (1998), 51-72.
6. Quoted in Derek Attig, "On the Occupy Wall Street Library," https://www.hastac.org/blogs/derekattig/2011/12/06/occupy-wall-street-library See also https://peopleslibrary.wordpress.com. Both last accessed 6-22-2020.
7. Steven K. Ashby and Robert Bruno, *A Fight for the Soul of Public Education: The Story of the Chicago Teacher's Strike* (Ithaca: Cornell University Press, 2016), p. 62.
8. Chuck Collins, Omar Ocampo, and Sophia Paslaski, "Billionaire Bonanza 2020: Wealth, Windfalls, Tumbling Taxes and Pandemic Profiteers" (The Institute for Policy Studies, 2020), pp. 1, 10.
9. United Nations, "Word Social Report 2020: Inequality in a Rapidly Changing World," p. 3.
10. Ta-Nehisi Coates, "The Enduring Solidarity of Whiteness," *The Atlantic*, February 8, 2016, emphasis the author's.
11. Ron Ramdin, *The Making of the Black Working Class in Britain* (Gower: 1987), page numbers not recoverable due to COVID library closure.
12. Nor was 1981 the end of Black resistance in the streets. For a visual archive of unrest in Birmingham and London in 1985 see John Akomfrah and the Black Audio Film Collective, *Handsworth Songs* (1986).
13. Ashley Dennis, "The Black Women Who Launched the Original Anti-racist Reading List," https://www.washingtonpost.com/outlook/2020/06/18/black-women-who-launched-original-anti-racist-reading-list/ (last accessed 6-22-20).
14. Charlemae Rollins, *We Build Together; A Reader's Guide to Negro Life and Literature for Elementary and High School Use* (Chicago: National Council of Teachers of English, 1948).

15. Archie L. Dick, *The Hidden History of South Africa's Book and Reading Cultures* (University of Toronto Press, 2012), p. 103.
16. "Below is a list of books that we would like folks to donate for the drive. We are primarily interested in books by Black and poc (person of color) authors, featuring Black and poc characters," BlackLivesMatterCU https://blmcu.wordpress.com (last accessed 6-22-2020).
17. Kasonde Thomas Mukonde, "Reading and the Making of Student Activists in Soweto, 1968-76," M.A. Thesis, Univeristy of Witwatersrand, 2020.

Introduction

Radical Book History

E. P. Thompson and The Making of the English Working Class

Antoinette Burton

Radically Bookish: The Afterlives of *The Making of the English Working Class*

This special issue on E. P. Thompson's *The Making of the English Working Class* (1963) grew out of a symposium I organized at the University of Illinois, Urbana-Champaign in October 2013 to commemorate the fiftieth anniversary of the book's publication. I am, on the face of it, one of the least likely modern British historians to be organizing such an event. I can remember the first time I held the weighty tome in my hands: I was a junior in college, in the fall of 1982, and it was on the syllabus for a course I was taking on Victorian Britain, taught by Jonathan Schneer at Yale University. As did many feminist and postcolonial historians of my generation, I struggled with what I saw as Thompson's indifference to women and gender (oh, those deluded followers of Joanna Southcott!) and his incapacity to see the evidence of race and empire in his sources even when they cried out from below the footnote line for all to see.

In the interim, a good many careers have been given over to defending, embracing, overturning, and tweaking the monumental claims made by this monumental book, the result of at least a decade of archival research and methodological rethinking. *The Making* was and is a palimpsest, a rich and textured parchment that has been scraped and used again. It has passed through so many hands that it has become a kind of recycled commons: shared if not fully subscribed to by multiple users who, whether they reject it or extend it or only read the preface, accord it an often storied status in their intellectual formation. Indeed, there have been a raft of conferences large and small in the past two years dedicated to wrestling with the questions raised by Thompson's big book and by extension, by his larger body of work—evidence of *The Making*'s long life and its role in shaping the intellectual lives of several generations of readers.

I would not say I have made my peace with *The Making*. Rather, teaching it as I have off and on in the 1990s and 2000s has given me a renewed appreciation for its durability and for its capacity to call out and make audible the specificities of whatever present moment in which it is being read. Teaching parts of the book in the fall of 2009 as the detritus of the global fiscal crisis fell all around us, hearing, perhaps for the first time, the historically particular iteration of humanism that shapes his account of working class politics, was especially poignant—and particularly so for scholars of my generation, for whom humanism has not, perhaps, felt like an intellectual desideratum or an ethical desideratum for a very long time. Like all radical history worth its salt, Thompson's work still has a lot to show us, as much about the present as about the pasts he so painstakingly evokes in *The Making*.

The articles presented here are less about Thompson the man or even Thompson the historian than they are about *The Making of the English Working Class* as a *book* itself. The bookish-ness of our collective project feels especially urgent. It seems important, in other words, at this juncture in the history of the book itself as a form, whether virtual or real, to be reminded that Thompson's book was here, and still is. Its monumentality alone secures for it a significant, if not permanent, place in history and historiography alike. But we nominated it for reconsideration on the occasion of its fiftieth anniversary because though—as with all those whose anniversaries and birthdays we fete—it has had a good run, we are not quite sure how long it will last. Will it be here in ten years time, in twenty? Will it remain, and in what form, after we who are gathered to witness its work in the world are gone? Are the ways it resonates now predictors of its long-term fate? Does its value reside chiefly in its function as an allegory for the politics and thinking of its time—and as a palimpsest for ours? Here its radical bookishness is key, for it hails the past and the present and the dynamic relationship between the two. That was a dynamic that Thompson well understood. Yet the pressure of contemporary history on the writing of the past remains a radical claim. As both an intellectual project and as a material object, then, *The Making* has weight. It is that weight, rather than a rehearsal of its arguments or contents, that contributors to this volume were asked to consider. In the articles that follow, scholars engage *The Making* as a storehouse of histories past and as a physical object: something that was materialized in print, that circulated and was consumed, carried around like so much baggage, refit and repurposed and likely, yes, at least in its original hardcover edition, even used as a doorstop. Beyond its contents, it matters as material culture: as a hefty, adamantine object whose future trend lines are uncertain because this is the age of the disappearance of just such books, at least in their form between two covers.

Any discussion of *The Making* today is surely elegiac because so few readers the world over will hold books like it in their hands, going forward. They will not feel the weight of history in the way that it has long been possible to do, not for all, but for some, in global terms. No Kindle book will deliver history in that historically specific way and, I daresay, no Kindle book works so well as a doorstop either. E-readers offer many other possibilities, but the touch of finger on paper, the vulnerability to the pencil mark, the signature of the author him- or herself, the sheer bulk and heaviness of mountains of tracts and pamphlets read and cited, digested and regurgitated—these are things that *The Making* archives, for now. With the book in hand, one feels the labor of this particular archive story. And one remembers what a struggle social history had to register as legitimate history, so that the book's very heft is evidence of how it had to prove its mettle against the traditional narratives it aimed to challenge.

Our engagement with *The Making of the English Working Class* at the symposium and in the essays below was the culumination of three years of thinking about "world histories from below"—a concept at least partially indebted to Thompsonian social history. We began by creating a shared vocabulary about the "global" and the "below"; then, under the intellectual leadership of Kathy Oberdeck, we moved to exploring the ways in which regular people, from shack dwellers to slaves to urban workers, demanded a role in shaping the structure of their worlds, especially around shelter, sanitation, and services. In the context of the Thompson anniversary, we focused on the entanglements of the natural world, capitalism, and public space as subjects of "grassroots" history.

In the retrospective shadow of *The Making*, all of the 2013 events surrounding the book (ours included) look a little belated: we are all engaged in a re-visioning of Thompson's and other Left historians' mid-twentieth-century commitment to the below that tells us as much about our present conditions as about any pasts we wish to recover. What we learned in these three years by thinking through world history from the bottom up is not that there is no accessible below, or that there is no a priori global, but that the meanings of both have to be talked through, argued about, and debated because these questions are never settled.

What is impressive is how Thompson's book continues to be one fulcrum for such engagement. What was unanticipated for me, personally, was how surprising it is that *The Making* has the capacity to tap into and re-reconfirm our desire for history, capital H—*even* allowing for our dissatisfaction with it, and *even* allowing for all the skepticism and paranoia that any engagement with a discipline like History entails.[1] Coming to terms not simply with the variety of impacts the book has had but also with the equal variety of intellectual, political, personal, and even visceral *experiences* it set into motion is itself a consequence of Thompson's own preoccupation with the kind of consciousness that he believed shaped collectivities in symbolic and material ways.

James Barrett starts us off with the long view of *The Making*'s influence, specifically by setting out the impact it had on US radical thinking at a formative moment in the country's history. For Barrett the socialist humanism of that time was a profoundly emotional experience as well as a professional and political one—a point that echoes the powerfully personal ways in which many people tend to remember their own encounters with *The Making*. In Ann Curthoys's article we see how *The Making* actually traveled—and how it did not—to Australia, following the histories of those whose radical protest took them to new shores and involved them in white settler histories of the kind Thompson himself scarcely took notice of. She reminds us of the battles between Thompson and George Rudé and of the range of social histories beyond *The Making* that seemed to serve the needs of antipodean histories better. Taken together, these first two pieces remind us of the material/ist histories of radicalism—as both a set of utopian possibilities and as a set of more unevenly lived experiences—that *The Making* intersected and helped to shape.

Chris Boyer asks challenging questions about the applicability of *The Making*'s concepts to the history of Mexico, focusing on Thompson's use of community to think about the portability of notions of class solidarity when looking at *pueblos* under the dictatorship of Porfirio Diaz. In so doing he does not so much challenge the universalism of Thompson's claims as he tests the viability of the moral economy and the social cohesion of peasants under the pressure of modernization and ultimately, revolution. Looking at the imperial project from another perspective, Zach Sell poses a question: "In what ways did the English working class fantasize about the American South and colonial India?" His answer, which draws as much on W. E. B. Du Bois as it does on Thompson, focuses on the "world-conquering visions" of slave masters and the movement of capital and bodies between zones of factory and plantation production. Indeed, in the wake of critical race history and postcolonial studies, the absence of attention to race in *The Making* has preoccupied scholars. Some like Ron Ramdin, have sought equivalencies, as in his 1987 *The Making of the Black Working Class in Britain*. Caroline

Bressey shows us how one might remain grounded in the materialities of class and still capture the multiethnic histories of the late eighteenth and early nineteenth centuries that formed the basis of *The Making*. Using historical geography as a concept and a method, Bressey assesses the eruptions of race as a category and racialized subjects as agents that can be seen in the making of a presumptively white British working class that Thompson's book archives. In the process, she calls for a reintegration of so-called black British geographies into transnational narratives of British modernity, a landscape that the life and work of the late Victorian radical reformer Catherine Impey so deftly illustrates.

Like Bressey and Sell and Boyer do here, many scholars have sought to map Thompson's concept of class and consciousness and feeling onto earlier centuries. Others, like Barrett and Curthoys, track the influence of *The Making* forward into the histories and historiographies that followed on from the 1960s. By contrast, Lara Kriegel pulls us into the very moment that the book was written in order to help us appreciate the affective contours of late 1950s Britain, specifically with reference to the "kitchen sink dramas" of the day. She reads texts like John Osborne's *Look Back in Anger* to recover the anomie and sense of hopelessness to be found in the recessive spaces of working class culture at the dawn of post-imperial Britain. In films and texts of the day, the household is a key space where the emotional disappointments of normative proletarian life play out, and a nostalgia for earlier working-class days of the kind that Thompson wrote about is practically palpable in all its gendered forms.

Kriegel ends her article by noting that *The Making* still has the power to materialize that nostalgia, as is evident by its prominent display in the Tate bookshop during an L. S. Lowry exhibition. Conversely, Isabel Hofmeyr focuses her attention on the negative space around the materialized text: the margins—and marginalia—of the book itself. She lays *The Making* against Steve Biko's posthumous compilation, *I Write What I Like*, arguing that they belong to the same reading formations. Each of these oppositional intellectuals hailed readers who engaged passionately with their writings and left indexical traces of their experience of the texts in the marginalia. Those scribblings leave, in turn, a fugitive, ghostly archive of reader response. Copies stolen or overdue, mysterious scratching, even outright theft—these are the archival traces Hofmeyr excavates.

Lest we fetishize the fiftieth anniversary moment, Utathya Chattopadhyaya reminds us of how the legacy of *The Making* unfolded twenty years after its publication, in the 1983 film *Talking History*. The film, produced by H. O. Nazareth and with a soundtrack by Spartacus R, puts Thompson in conversation with C. L. R. James at a pivotal moment in the history of internationalism—and in Thatcher's multiracial Britain as well. There are no one-to-one correspondences between *The Making* and the film, but as Chattopadhyaya points out, James's controlled, witty criticism of the insular European left in the face of eruptions of Third World political rebellion across the globe—eruptions effectively captured by the cut-and-paste newspaper clippings Nazareth's film throws up—reminds us of how resoundingly self-aware Thompson was, yet how deaf he could also be to radical cosmopolitan forms beyond his ken. This, together with the contrapuntal rhythms of Spartacus R's music, underscores the contradictions between the Little Englander character of *The Making* with Thompson's own particular politics of internationalism.

As we track Thompson's influence in a variety of locations, genres, and reading communities, the limits and possibilities of that peculiar politics are in very much evidence in the articles that follow. Most of the contributors do not do a close reading of *The Making*; they are more interested in what it has meant to various communities, how it shaped narratives, and how it has reflected the times in which it was written, for better or for worse. If they demonstrate how Thompson's tome remains radically bookish, they are not hagiographical, not by any means. But they do ask what *The Making* means now and that very question is a form of homage. In that sense, they testify, however unwittingly, to the outsized impact of this big book not just on readers who have encountered it in various ways, but on the way historians and literary scholars and many others besides think about community, about reading practice, about class and its multiform histories in the long shadow Thompson's work has left. Taken together, our reflections suggest that, contemporary anxieties about the fate of the book itself as an embodied medium of history notwithstanding—despite the short-term crisis of bookishness in general, in other words—*The Making* remains an enduring artifact of both English history as it was and the social and cultural history of the book form as we know it.

Notes

1. I draw here on Alan Berube, *My Desire for History: Essays in Gay, Community and Labor History* (Chapel Hill: University of North Carolina Press, 2011).

Chapter 1

Making and Unmaking the Working Class

E. P. Thompson and the "New Labor History" in the United States

James R. Barrett

The Indian historian Rajnarayan Chandavarkar recalled a most unusual salute to a most unusual book. "In the late 1970s, when E. P. Thompson was elected President of the Indian History Congress, and rode into session on the back of an elephant, this was a tribute primarily to *The Making,*" a book the Canadian historian Bryan Palmer calls "arguably the most influential book in the modern historiography of working-class studies."[1] At the time of Thompson's death, E. J. Hobsbawm noted that he was cited more than any other historian in the twentieth century.[2] For more than a generation, *The Making* has shaped historical writing throughout the world,[3] including in societies very different from Thompson's own.[4] Perhaps the greatest paradox, however, is that although Thompson's work defined the "working class" for a generation, it also helped to deconstruct the very notion of class itself, and nowhere was this more true than in the United States.

Socialist Humanism and Radical History in the United States

It is impossible to understand Thompson's book and why it appeared when it did without considering the political and intellectual context that he reacted against—on the one hand, a determinist form of European Marxism and on the other, the structuralist form of contemporary sociology, wherein class became a quantifiable category via modernization theory.[5] Likewise, the peculiar trajectory of the postwar American Left helps to explain the warm embrace of *The Making*. The ideological fit between Thompson's Socialist Humanism and "looser" conceptions of class formation and those of a new generation of left intellectuals was strongest in the United States in the late 1960s and the 1970s, when the new labor history was gestating.[6]

One way to gauge the book's effect is to contrast its distance from an earlier generation of American radical historians. The main contribution of the older group, which coalesced around the journal *Studies on the Left*, was the notion of a "corporate liberal" consensus that held sway through much of the twentieth century.[7] This group went through graduate school in the late 1950s and early 1960s and had connections with the Old Left but was "notable for its heterodoxy," in part at least because of the catastrophic decline of the postwar Left and the weak tradition of Marxist scholarship in the United States.[8] Most viewed history—and American politics—from the top down and analyzed corporate executives and foreign policy makers, but their work also included Eugene Genovese's studies of the Southern planter elite. When they considered workers at all, it was largely in negative terms. The failure of immigrant workers to develop a class conscious labor movement bred disorganization and social pathologies ranging from insanity to crime and alcoholism. They were, Gabriel Kolko concluded, "lumpen people in a lumpen society." This group's most important conclusion, historian Jon Weiner notes, "was that virtually all popular and protest movements had been incorporated within the expanding capitalist system, instead of undermining it."[9]

By the late 1960s, a very different orientation and group of historians emerged. With the publication of *Radical America* beginning in 1967, the political and historiographical tables were turned. The journal championed agency, spontaneity, and working-class and slave self-activity. "The Marxism *Radical America* adopted was the unorthodox variant developed by E. P. Thompson," Peter Novick writes, "a Marxism that valued working-class culture and consciousness and strove to integrate class analysis with the cultural concerns growing out of black nationalism, feminism, and youth culture."[10] Novick misses the decisive influence of the West Indian scholar C. L. R. James who brought a popular culture angle and an insistence on the centrality of race, but there is no mistaking Thompson's impact.[11] *Radical America* published socialist feminist writing from factories and community organizations as well as studies of women's, working-class, and black history. The *Radical History Review* was also deeply influenced by the new labor history and carried the banner of radical history throughout the late 1970s and 1980s.

This younger group tapped into the insights of two older scholars who were influenced by and shared some experiences with Thompson. David Montgomery and Herbert Gutman both had backgrounds in the Old Left, though Gutman had exited from the movement while he was still young. After a decade in industrial work, Montgomery left the Communist Party in the mid-1950s, around the same time as Thompson: both had come to believe that the organization was increasingly irrelevant to radical politics. Montgomery's work reflected his industrial experiences, focusing on gritty studies of the workplace, strike activity, and working-class politics. Gutman's background in the radical Jewish culture of New York shaped his sensitivity to local working-class cultures. Both scholars sought to connect their research and that of their students with the labor movement.[12]

The "New Labor Historians" and *The Making of the English Working Class*

It is difficult to over-state the hunger for an approach that at once promised common people a place in the historical narrative and provided a model that captured the complexity of their experience. In Thompson, these historians found a theory of class formation more compatible with their own loose understandings of the term and one that focused on everyday lives. "*The Making of the English Working Class* resonated perfectly with the hopes of a generation of radical scholars that common people could make their own history," Alan Dawley argued. "In the United States the book was quickly assimilated to a radical populism which aimed at doing history 'from the bottom up' to show that the poor ... made history on their own terms."[13] Leaving aside the legacy of the Cold War, these labor historians were working against an entrenched Whig tradition that focused on labor institutions, emphasizing the virtue of the business union model while rejecting any notion of "social unionism." They also faced the *Studies* group's emphasis on the decisive power and influence of American capital—whether in the persons of paternalist slave masters or cosmopolitan "corporate liberals." There was little role for common workers, slave or free, in either story.

The new approach provided a sweeping reinterpretation of what Thompson termed the historical "presence" of common people. Montgomery demonstrated the impact of workers on the broader history of industrialization, liberalism, and the evolution of the American state and imperialism. Though most remembered for his workplace studies, which might seem distant from *The Making*'s narrative, he was greatly influenced both by Thompson's notion of the pervasive influence of class and by his insistence on workers' agency. Where Thompson had focused on a literate and articulate group of artisan radicals, the key group in Montgomery's "project" of class consciousness was the "militant minority"—a group of syndicalists, socialists, and progressive unionists who sought to bring their workmates together into an aggressive labor movement. Focusing mainly on male workers, Montgomery probed the gendered character of skilled work cultures, considered both race and ethnicity as vital to understanding the evolution of working-class identity, and absorbed, fitfully, the efforts of feminists and others who were attempting to deconstruct the archetypical worker as a white, skilled male.[14]

Looking at Montgomery, Gutman, and the younger group that followed in their wake establishes the profound influence of Thompson and *The Making* on a generation of scholars who transformed our understanding of US social history. At first, the new field was shaped primarily by reactions to older approaches, notably the large body of work associated with the labor economists John R. Commons and Selig Perlman.[15] Both Montgomery's *Beyond Equality,* which placed workers at the center of Civil War and Reconstruction politics, and some of Gutman's pioneering studies of local working-class cultures, had already appeared before the authors became aware of *The Making*.[16]

Yet in each case Thompson's book transformed the author's understanding of the field. Gutman's collaborator Ira Berlin writes that it stimulated Gutman to conceptualize his local studies in terms of class formation. "Thompson's understanding of class ... and of class consciousness as the cultural articulation of those experiences, was also Gutman's," Berlin wrote, "[and his] ... overarching commitment to empirical research [was] also Thompson's ... it was not so much the emphasis on culture that drew him to Thompson as it was Thompson's ... outright celebration of human agency." Gutman brilliantly captured the need of industrialists to transform not only the technology and methods of production, but also the culture and work habits of the people involved.[17] Thompson had shown that this was an uneven, complex, and contentious process in England; Gutman showed that it was far more complex in the United States because of migration, race, and ethnicity.

The Making's deepest and most enduring mark on the American narrative concerned the eighteenth-century plebian Atlantic world. While Marcus Rediker and Peter Linebaugh followed Thompson in their brilliant evocation of the remarkably diverse and insurrectionary early modern maritime world, Al Young established the agency of artisans, the crowd, and the working poor in the context of the American Revolution.[18]

It is not surprising then that the earliest Thompsonesque studies focused on a comparable period in the United States, and for a while it seemed that he provided an admirable model for the history of early industrialization. A generation of young Yankee farmwomen constituted America's first factory proletariat in New England's textile towns, facing the sort of rigors of industrial work Thompson had described. They mixed with British and native-born skilled workers as well as a population of laboring poor, including free and enslaved blacks, to constitute the original American working-class population. By the 1830s, a labor movement and a class culture and politics resembling the one in Thompson's narrative emerged in numerous cities—trades unions, cooperatives, Working Men's institutes, political parties, newspapers, and a small group of organic intellectuals advocating a new perspective on political economy that emphasized a labor theory of value.[19] As Thompson's artisans had done with the rights of the freeborn Englishmen, they reworked the ideology of the early republic, creating a "labor republicanism" and demanding not only better wages, but also shorter hours, universal free education, and other reforms aimed at making the United States a more egalitarian society.[20]

The process was perhaps most advanced in Philadelphia, where the General Trades Union (GTU) drew in more than fifty organizations representing laborers and factory operatives as well as artisans from diverse backgrounds—more than ten thousand workers in all. When the unskilled coal heavers walked off the job over long hours, artisans stopped work too, declaring, "We are all day laborers." In 1835 a huge general strike for shorter hours commenced, involving as many as twenty thousand—far beyond the boundaries of the expansive GTU.[21] The moment of class formation, it seemed, had arrived, and at about the same moment as the Chartist revolt, Thompson's point of class maturation in England. Yet within a few years this promising movement had been destroyed and workers were bitterly divided along ethnic, racial, and religious lines.

Making and Unmaking the Working Class

One paradox in *The Making* towers over others and has particular relevance for the study of the United States, where other forms of constructed identity have tended to displace class as a key analytical category over the past generation. "[I]t is ironical that while Thompson was perhaps best known, and most widely admired, for having demonstrated how the history of a class may be written," Chandavarkar writes, "his method and style of argument may have contributed substantially to the deconstruction and dissolution of the very concept of class."[22] Thompson's emphasis on the diversity of working-class experience, his insistence on the rootedness of class in particular sites and cultures, his "loosening" of our understanding of class—shifting the stuff of causation from structures and modes of production to experience and agency—have paradoxically led to an emphasis on fragmentation.

The precision of class as a category of analysis dissolved as historians' evocation of class experience became increasingly detailed and complex and as Thompson's artisan-based movement appeared more and more unusual over time, particularly in societies like the United States that were characterized increasingly by massive rural and transnational migration and by mass production technologies. In other societies as well, gender, race, and other forms of identity appeared vital to explaining the experience of workers and their roles in history. If we have deconstructed and greatly complicated the notions of class and class formation, this process started not with postmodern theory but rather with *The Making*.

This process of deconstruction relates in part to chronology. A possibility that Thompson did not consider in *The Making* is the idea that class formation is never complete and that laboring people never permanently constitute a "mature" working class. Rather, the historical experience and "presence" of a working class is best conveyed through a dynamic process of formation and fragmentation over time. Even in the UK, Hobsbawm, Stedman Jones, and others emphasized the ongoing process of class formation and argued that if there were a *distinct* era in which the English working class "made," it was likely long after Thompson's 1830s.[23]

In the United States, fragmentation was particularly striking. Within a decade of America's first labor movement in the 1830s, its cities were increasingly overwhelmed by a tide of immigrants, above all, by the Irish. Thompson's own discussion of the Irish in the industrial towns of northern England began to suggest divergent class experiences based on ethnicity. Since immigrants represented a much larger proportion of the laboring population in the country, the significance of ethnicity was far more pronounced in America, where nativist movements swept the society and promising local labor movements splintered along ethnic and religious lines. In Philadelphia Catholic and Protestant weavers who had helped to create the city's vibrant GTU and waged the successful general strike of 1835 now turned on one another in streets and workplaces over which version of the bible was the proper one for Philadelphia's school children. In the wake of economic depression, religious sectarianism, and attacks from employers' organizations, the institutional framework for urban working-class society in the United States was largely destroyed. The American narrative looked much more like an "unmaking" than a "making."[24]

This issue of ethnic and racial difference loomed far larger from the late nineteenth century through the early twentieth, with massive waves of "New Immigrants" who came in larger numbers and from a wider range of societies than the "Old Immigrants" of the mid-nineteenth century. Italians, Poles, Russian and East European Jews and others each created their own communities and cultures, greatly complicating the task of those seeking to weld them together into an effective working-class movement. As people of color migrated to American industrial cities from Asia, the American South, and Mexico, racial conflict loomed. In the early twentieth century, racial conflagrations tore apart even the most promising organizational efforts. European immigrant workers and their children toiled alongside Blacks and Latinos, fashioning their own identities and institutional and cultural lives amidst this ethnic and racial diversity, while retaining some sense of their distinct cultures.[25] Gutman conceptualized this process as one of interaction between these successive waves of migrants and the evolving fabric of an urban industrial society. Each generation of migrants faced anew Thompson's trauma of industrial work discipline and the process of class formation.[26] Each generation of labor activists faced the challenge by either excluding the newcomers or by developing strategies to bring their constituents together across ethnic lines. The problem in the United States was not that the working class never was "made," but rather that it was "remade" continuously.

Labor History's "Race Problem"

The key difference between Thompson's narrative and what happened in the United States concerns race. It was not simply a matter of distinct communities organized along racial and ethnic lines. Rather, the process of working-class formation itself was racialized. White workers developed a sense of class identity that led them to define, organize, and mobilize "Labor" in racial terms, and this process was as intimately linked to slavery as to wage labor and also to the influx of Asian and even many European migrants who were viewed as less-than-white. So long as historians saw the wage and slave labor systems and the workers engaged in them as separate and distinct, which was often the case until the early 1990s, this was less of a problem. But, of course, they were not separate in the labor market or in the minds of white and black workers. Notions of agency and slave community and culture emerged as major themes, particularly in the work of George Rawick, but for a generation, the study of slaves and their lives tended to be seen as a separate field. This prevented labor historians from grasping the full complexity of working-class formation in the United States. A capacious approach to class still tended to compartmentalize and neglect a large population of the most exploited elements in the working-class population.[27]

David Roediger, whose own approach was deeply influenced by Thompson but even more by W. E. B. Du Bois, looked at precisely the Thompsonian moment in the US, from the late eighteenth through mid-nineteenth century. He employed a similar approach and many of the same kinds of sources, but he carried Thompson's argument about working-class agency one step further to explain the racialized character of class formation in the United States. As in England, American workers were active agents in their own making as a class, but the identity was one of a *white working class*. It is yet another testament to *The Making*'s influence that perhaps the most searching critique of the "new labor history" is framed largely in terms of Thompson's approach and particularly his argument regarding workers' agency. In this case, however, Roediger argued that "whiteness," like class, was a constructed, not a natural identity, that American workers were active agents in the creation of a *white* working-class identity, and that it was impossible to separate class formation from this process of racial formation.[28]

Some see Roediger's determination to document the agency of white workers in creating and reproducing racism as crowding out the role of the ruling class in this process. It also now seems that the working-class abolitionists, who included many German immigrants, were likely a larger group than he had realized. Some white labor activists saw abolition and labor reform as part of the same democratic vision.[29]

Nevertheless, most labor historians came to acknowledge that race was inextricably linked to class formation and fragmentation; that the gradual and uneven formation of a class identity was interwoven with that of a racial identity; and that white racism was perhaps the most serious obstacle, among many, to the formation of class consciousness. If it were proper to speak of an American working class, this could not be used in the same way the term was applied in *The Making*. Even for its portrayal of England, however, *The Making* has been criticized for achieving its definition and narrative of class only by ignoring issues of social difference, notably gender, and for failing to weigh the significance of England's imperial status.[30] As in the United States, race was certainly a vital element in various colonial settings and even in the UK.

The Emotional Dimension

Where are we headed today and what, if anything, does a new trajectory have to do with Thompson's book? It was concerned to convey what class felt like: to endure factory work; to be politically marginalized and excluded; to have one's children denied a proper education and instead sentenced to a life of hard labor at an early age. Thompson recognized what many historians seem still not to have learned—that class is not only a material, social, and cultural experience, but is also in a profound sense emotional. What we call class consciousness, as a sort of shorthand, involved not only social and political aspirations, but also a world of hurt, resentment, and anger.[31] Without emotions, the element of *experience* at the heart of Thompson's analysis recedes. Emotions seem a world away from the frameworks most social historians employ. Yet if culture was the medium through which working people "handled" class, it was experienced at the personal level and shared socially through emotions.[32]

This may not be precisely what Thompson meant when he used Raymond Williams's phrase "structures of feeling," but there is no doubt that at numerous places in his own book, the affective side of class is evoked to demonstrate the personal as well as the social costs of industrial work, political exclusion, class discrimination. When he reached for a metaphor to convey the pervasive but elusive quality of class experience, Thompson invoked emotions. "The finest-meshed sociological net cannot give us a pure specimen of class," he wrote, "any more than it can give us one of deference or love."[33]

Toward the end of his life, Thompson found it difficult to prescribe any particular approach, to establish an "Agenda for Radical History," to define his own relationship to Marxism. Instead, he spoke of human needs and emotions and the implications of these for creating a radical history: "I find a lot in the Marxist tradition … marked by what is ultimately a capitalist definition of human need … in economic material terms, [which] tends to enforce a hierarchy of causation which affords insufficient priority to other needs: the needs of identity, the needs of gender identity, the need for respect and status among working people themselves."[34]

We revisit Thompson's book not simply to decide whether or not he got the story right; it has always been as much a political statement as a scholarly interpretation. On the political side, his Socialist Humanism resonated with a generation of scholars looking to break with Cold War liberalism and highly structuralist forms of Marxism; this form of socialism continues to shape the values and perspectives of many social historians in the United States and elsewhere. In terms of labor scholarship, his looser conception of class formation provided a framework for understanding the complexity of the process in America, where racial and ethnic identity undermined the growth of class awareness and organization. The irony that this new approach to class making led to a greater appreciation for un-making, however, has not reduced the continuing significance of Thompson's book for the rest of us. We continue to read it to better understand the power relations in our past and present and to make a mark upon our own disciplines and on our societies—as actors in a broader humanity that resides at the center of *The Making*.

James Barrett, *Professor Emeritus of History and African American Studies at the University of Illinois at Urbana-Champaign and Scholar in Residence at The Newberry Library, is the author of* The Irish Way: Becoming American in the Multiethnic City *(Penguin, 2012) and* From the Bottom, Up and the Inside, Out: Race, Ethnicity, and Identity in Working Class History *(Duke University Press, 2017). With Jenny Barrett, he is working on* Chicago: A Peoples' History.

Notes

For helpful comments, thanks to Jenny Barrett, Bryan Palmer, David Roediger, Leon Fink, and Bruce Levine.

1. Rajnarayan Chandavarkar, "The Making of the Working Class: E. P. Thompson and Indian History," *History Workshop Journal* 43 (Spring 1997): 179.
2. "E. P. Thompson Obituary," *Independent*, 30 August 1993, cited in Bryan D. Palmer, "Homage to Edward Thompson," Part II, *Labour/LeTravail* 33 (Spring 1994): 14n2. See also, E. J. Hobsbawm, *Interesting Times: A Twentieth Century Life* (New York: Pantheon Books, 2002), 214.
3. Frederick Cooper, "Work, Class and Empire: An African Historian's Retrospective on E. P. Thompson," *Social History* 20, no. 2 (May 1995): 235–241; Chandavarkar, "The Making of the Working Class," 177–196.

4. Chandavarkar, "The Making of the Working Class"; Bryan Palmer, "Paradox and Polemic; Argument and Awkwardness: Reflections on E. P. Thompson," Keynote address delivered at the "Fifty Years of *The Making of the English Working Class,*" University of London, 25 June 2013.
5. Scott Hamilton, *The Crisis of Theory: E. P. Thompson, the New Left and Postwar British Politics* (Manchester: Manchester University Press, 2011), 49–226; Perry Anderson, *Arguments within English Marxism* (London: New Left Books, 1980); Palmer, *E. P. Thompson*, 69–86.
6. The "loose" characterization is from William Sewell, "How Classes Are Made: Critical Reflections on E. P. Thompson's Theory of Working-Class Formation," in *E. P. Thompson*, ed. Kaye and McClelland, 54–56.
7. Gabriel Kolko, *The Triumph of Conservatism: A Reinterpretation of American History* (New York: Free Press, 1963); James Weinstein, *The Corporate Ideal in the Liberal State* (Boston: Beacon Press, 1968); James Weinstein and David Eakins, eds., *For a New America: Essays in History and Politics from Studies on the Left* (New York: Vintage Books, 1970).
8. Peter Novick, *That Noble Dream: The "Objectivity Question" and the American Historical Profession* (Cambridge: Cambridge University Press, 1988), 424. See also, Paul Buhle, *History and the New Left: Madison, Wisconsin, 1950–1970* (Philadelphia: Temple University Press, 1990).
9. Gabriel Kolko, *Main Currents in Modern American History* (New York: Harper and Row, 1977), 99; Jonathon M. Weiner, "Radical Historians and the Crisis in American History, 1959–1980," *Journal of American History* 76, no. 2 (September 1989): 408.
10. Novick, *That Noble Dream*, 424.
11. Peter Linebaugh, "What if C. L. R. James Had Met E. P. Thompson in 1792?" *Urgent Tasks*, no. 12 (Summer 1981): 108–110 brings Thompson and James together in creative ways.
12. James R. Barrett, "Class Act: An Interview with David Montgomery," *Labor: Studies in Working-Class History of the Americas* 1, no. 1 (2004): 25–57; Weiner, "Radical Historians," 410–412; "Interview with Herbert Gutman," in Herbert G. Gutman, *Power and Culture: Essays on the American Working Class*, ed. Ira Berlin (New York: Pantheon, 1987), 329–356.
13. Alan Dawley, "E. P. Thompson and the Peculiarities of the Americans," *Radical History Review* no. 19 (Winter 1978–79): 39. See also Sean Wilentz, *Chants Democratic: New York City and the Rise of the American Working Class, 1780–1850*, 2nd ed. (New York: Oxford University Press, 2004), xii–xiii.
14. "Remembering David Montgomery (1926–2011), His Scholarship, and His Mentorship," *Labour/Le Travail* 70 (Fall 2012): 203–223. See also Elizabeth Faue, "Retooling the Class Factory: United States Labour History after Marx, Montgomery, and Postmodernism," *Labour History* 82 (May 2002): 109–119.
15. John R. Commons et al., *History of Labor in the United States*, 4 vols. (New York: Macmillan, 1918–1935); Selig Perlman, *A Theory of the Labor Movement* (New York: Macmillan, 1928); David Brody, "The Old Labor and the New: In Search for an American Working Class," *Labor History* 20, no. 1 (Winter 1979): 11–126; Leon Fink, "John R. Commons, Herbert Gutman, and the Burden of Labor History," *Labor History* 29, no. 3 (1988): 313–322.
16. David Brody, "David Montgomery, Field Builder," *Labor: Studies in Working-Class History of the Americas* 10, no. 1 (Spring 2013): 53–56; James R. Barrett, "Class

Act: An Interview with David Montgomery," *Labor: Studies in Working-Class History of the Americas* 1, no. 1 (2004): 25–57; "Interview with Herbert Gutman."

17. Ira Berlin, "Introduction," in Gutman, *Power and Culture*, 18, 19.
18. Peter Linebaugh and Marcus Rediker, *The Many-Headed Hydra: Sailors, Slaves, Commoners, and the Hidden History of the Revolutionary Atlantic* (Boston: Beacon Press, 2000); Alfred F. Young, *The Shoemaker and the Tea Party: Memory and the American Revolution* (Boston: Beacon Press, 1999).
19. Alan Dawley, *Class and Community: The Industrial Revolution in Lynn* (Cambridge: Harvard University Press, 1976); Bruce Laurie, *The Working People of Philadelphia, 1800–1850* (Philadelphia: Temple University Press, 1980); Wilentz, *Chants Democratic*; David Montgomery, "The Working Classes of the Preindustrial City, 1780–1830," *Labor History* 9, no. 1 (1983): 3–22.
20. David Montgomery, *Beyond Equality: Labor and the Radical Republicans, 1862–1872* (New York: Alfred A. Knopf, 1967); Leon Fink, "The New Labor History of the Powers of Historical Pessimism: Consensus, Hegemony, and the Case of the Knights of Labor," *Journal of American History* 75, no. 1 (June 1988): 116.
21. *Pennsylvanaian*, June 4, 1835 as quoted in Laurie, *The Working People of Philadelphia*, 91.
22. Chandavarkar, "The Making of the Working Class," 177.
23. Eric Hobsbawm, "The Making of the Working Class," in *Workers: Worlds of Labor*, ed. Eric Hobsbawm (New York: Pantheon, 1984), 194–213; Gareth Stedman Jones, "Working-Class Culture and Working-Class Politics in London, 1870–1900: Notes on the Remaking of a Working Class," *Journal of Social History* 7, no. 4 (Summer 1974): 498–500. See also Anderson, *Arguments within English Marxism*, 43–49.
24. Laurie, *The Working People of Philadelphia*; David Montgomery, "The Shuttle and the Cross: Weavers and Artisans in the Kensington Riots of 1844," *Journal of Social History* 5, no. 4 (1972): 411–466.
25. James R. Barrett, "The World of the Worker," in *Oxford Handbook of Immigration History*, ed. Ronald Bayor (New York: Oxford University Press, 2014); James R. Barrett, "Unity and Fragmentation: Class, Race, and Ethnicity on Chicago's South Side, 1900–1922," *Journal of Social History* 18, no. 1 (1984): 37–56.
26. Herbert Gutman, "Work, Culture, and Society in Industrializing America, 1815–1919," in Gutman, *Work, Culture, and Society in Industrializing America: Essays in American Working-Class and Social History* (New York: Vintage Books, 1977).
27. Herbert Hill, "The Problem of Race in American Labor History," *Reviews in American History* 24, no. 2 (June 1996): 180–208; David Roediger, "Labor in White Skin: Race and Working Class History," in *The Year Left 3: Reshaping the US Left*, ed. Mike Davis and Michael Sprinker (London: Verso, 1988); George P. Rawick, *From Sundown to Sunup: The Making of the Black Community* (Westport, CT: Greenwood, 1972); Eugene D. Genovese, *Roll, Jordan, Roll: The World the Slaves Made* (New York: Pantheon Books, 1974).
28. David R. Roediger, *The Wages of Whiteness: Race and the Making of the American Working Class* (London: Verso, 1991).
29. Bruce Laurie, *Beyond Garrison: Antislavery and Social Reform* (Cambridge: Cambridge University Press, 2005). See also, Edward Magdol, *The Anti-Slavery Rank and File: A Social Profile of the Abolitionists' Constituency* (Westport, CT: Greenwood Press, 1986).
30. Joan Wallach Scott, "Women in The Making of the English Working Class," in Scott, *Gender and the Politics of History* (New York: Columbia University Press,

1988), 68–91; Anna Clark, *The Struggle for the Breeches: Gender and the Making of the British Working Class* (Berkeley: University of California Press, 1995); Robert Gregg, "Class, Culture, and Empire: E. P. Thompson and the Making of Social History," *Journal of Historical Sociology* 11, no. 4 (December 1998): 419–460.

31. Emotional elements of class remain largely unexplored by historians. For a treatment based on interviews in the late 1960s, see Richard Sennett and Jonathan Cobb, *The Hidden Injuries of Class* (New York: Random House, 1972).

32. "[It is] through the missing term, 'experience,' [that] structure is transmuted into process and the subject re-enters into history." E. P. Thompson, *The Poverty of Theory and Other Essays* (New York: Monthly Review Press, 1978), 170–171. Scott sees experience as an unexamined, essentialist concept, but the concept lies at the heart of Thompson's theory of class formation, and it remains a vital element in writing history from below. Presumably, it was this dedication to capturing the *experience* of class that led Thompson to acquire and learn how to operate a handloom. See Joan Wallach Scott, "Experience," in *Feminists Theorize the Political*, ed. Judith Butler and Joan Wallach Scott (New York: Routledge, 1992); William Sewell, "How Classes Are Made," 55–56, 59–65. On Thompson's handloom, see E. J. Hobsbawm, "Edward Palmer Thompson, 1924–1993," *Proceedings of the British Academy* 90 (1996): 524, as cited in Palmer, "Paradox and Polemic," 5.

33. Raymond Williams, *Problems in Materialism and Culture: Selected Essays* (London: New Left Books, 1980), 31–49; E. P. Thompson, *The Making of the English Working Class* (London: Gollancz, 1963), 9.

34. "Agenda for Radical History," in E. P. Thompson, *Making History: Writings on History and Culture* (New York: New Press, 1994), 362.

Chapter 2

History from Down Under

E. P. Thompson's The Making of the English Working Class *and Australia*

Ann Curthoys

Australia appears in *The Making of the English Working Class* as a distant and shadowy place, the site of punishment for British and Irish convicts through exile and forced labor. To be sent there is implicitly a kind of death. While Thompson has almost a dozen brief mentions of the sentencing of rioters, radicals, and rebels to transportation, he does not follow those so sentenced to the far corners of the earth. When they leave England, they disappear from his narrative. Yet productive and striking concepts can and do travel far. If Thompson did not follow his radicals to Australia's convict colonies, his major work came to influence the ways in which historians of Australia did history. And it was not only the historians: Thompson's work was important also for literary critics and scholars in a range of humanities disciplines, from anthropology to cultural studies and beyond.[1] Focusing here on those who researched and wrote specifically in the field of Australian history, we can see that *The Making*'s influence was slight in the 1960s and 1970s and reached a peak in the 1980s. It has remained important since, though its influence has declined as Indigenous and race-relations history, the new British imperial history, and transnational approaches came to the fore.

These Australian readings of *The Making* have a specific historical context. Thompson himself was energized by his times, affected by World War II and the Cold War. He wrote history to help him understand the English society in which he lived and which he both valued and sought to change. Australian historians have been influenced by their times too, by industrial conflict, new social movements, failed attempts to become a republic, debates over Indigenous pasts and futures, and much else. In tracing Thompson's antipodean historiographical influence, I'll also be exploring the connections between the historians' own times and the histories they wrote. Along the way, I also explore the work of Thompson's two contemporaries—Russel Ward and George Rudé—and ponder the significance of pathways chosen and avoided in creating the historiographical landscape we work in today.

The First Edition

When *The Making* appeared in 1963, historians of Australia were at first slow to respond. As one might expect, the book first aroused the interest of specialists in British and more broadly European history. At the University of Sydney, where I was a history student from 1963 to 1966, the teachers of British and European history—Ken Macnab and Barrie Rose—read *The Making* with interest. Macnab, an Australian who had been in England undertaking doctoral research at the University of Sussex when *The Making* appeared, arrived at Sydney in 1965 and began to use *The Making* in his honors course on working-class British history.[2] One of his students, Suzanne Bellamy, remembers that it was "a backbone text" in the course, and, she continues, "I still have my copy. There was a kind of romance about it even then."[3] Barrie Rose, a specialist in French Revolutionary history who had arrived from England at the University of Sydney in 1960, and who had published an essay two years earlier on eighteenth-century English food riots, was also keenly aware of Thompson's work.[4] It took longer for Thompson to be read by those specializing in Australian history, one reason being that the study of Australian history was still a fledgling enterprise compared with the lively world of British history that had nourished *The Making*.[5] At that time, history departments in Australian universities usually taught a great deal more British history than Australian, seeing the former as the foundation in any case of Australian history, and in some cases the latter as of little interest.

Though it took a while for historians of Australia to grow in numbers and to see *The Making*'s significance for their work, they were familiar with a somewhat similar book from one in their own ranks.[6] Only five years earlier Russel Ward's *The Australian Legend* had appeared. A drastically shortened and revised version of his seven hundred page PhD thesis completed at the Australian National University in 1956, it used folk ballads and similar sources to create a sense of the cultural world of Australian rural workers in the nineteenth century—convict, ex-convict and free. The parallels between the two historians are intriguing. Like Thompson, Ward had been a member of the Communist Party but had left in 1949, and he shared with Thompson a kind of Marxist humanism. Like Thompson, he had begun his scholarly life in literary studies, and moved to history somewhat later.[7] And like Thompson, his background was in literature as much as history; where Thompson had explored ideas of liberty and the rights of freeborn Englishmen, Ward explored the notion that harsh experiences and environment had produced in Australian rural workers a distinctive collectivist, egalitarian, anti-intellectual, independent, and democratic ethos.[8] Though both books were interested in working people's experience and identities, neither focused on the new industrial workers. Both were influenced by the 1950s and 1960s folk revival, which had provoked an interest in collecting old folk songs and studying the popular traditions that had nurtured them.[9] Ward, in particular, was influenced by British folklorists like Euan McColl and A. L. Lloyd, whose interests in turn included Australian folk songs.[10] They also shared an idea that was later to become significant for the fields of cultural studies and cultural history—the writings, songs, stories, and poems loved and reproduced by a specific group of people give us now some access to that group's cultural values and way of thinking.

Like *The Making*, *The Australian Legend* is still read and cited, though it, too, has been subject to extensive critique. While mainly remembered now by historians of Australia, at the time of its appearance it attracted the attention of scholars of comparative frontier history working in Canada and the United States who were interested, as Ward was, in Frederick Jackson Turner's "frontier thesis" postulating the creation of a distinctive American identity on the frontiers of settlement.[11] In the UK there was less interest, but Asa Briggs—the noted scholar of Victorian England—had in his chapter on Melbourne in *Victorian Cities* (1963), warmly described *The Australian Legend* as having "greatly enriched Australian historiography."[12]

Although so clear in retrospect, the similarities between the two books do not seem to have attracted written comments at the time. David Kent, an historian who migrated from England to Australia in 1975, partly inspired by having read *The Australian Legend* twelve years earlier, described it as a prime example of "history from below" before the term became popular, deserving of mention alongside those "three great scholars, George Rudé, Eric Hobsbawm, and Edward Thompson."[13] Kent sees Ward as a pioneer, as indeed he was, but it was to be some considerable time before his attention to popular culture and ordinary people took effect in Australian historiography, and when it did, those "three great scholars" were at least as influential as Ward.

At first, the interest in *The Making* for those historians working on Australian history was in Thompson's cast of insurgents and radicals, and what had happened to those among them who were transported to the colonies of New South Wales and Van Diemen's Land. The first direct published reference in Australian historiography to *The Making* that I have been able to find is in a three-page essay published in 1965 on "The Cato Street Conspirators in New South Wales" by a young Australian historian George Parsons. Parsons described *The Making*'s account of the Cato Street conspiracy of 1820 as "by far the best," and used it to describe the conspiracy as representing the last gasp of British Jacobin radicalism. His essay traced the subsequent lives of three of the five radicals who were transported, noting they became leading citizens (chief constable, tailor, and baker) in the town of Bathurst, west of Sydney, and suggested there was room for more research on Britain's transported radicals.[14] Parsons tells me that he wrote the essay directly as a response to reading *The Making*, which he had first encountered through Barrie Rose, his lecturer in European History, and a copy of which his Marxist mother had bought for him at great expense.[15]

Parsons, however, was unusual. The historians of convictism in the 1960s were generally not interested in Thompsonian radicals, but rather in the bulk of the convicts—160,000 of them—transported largely for crimes of theft. The issue that interested them was the long-standing one of the moral character of the convicts, centered on a question sometimes dubbed "victims or villains?" Were the convicts, in other words, the victims of Britain's agrarian and industrial revolutions, or were they hardened criminals transported as a last resort? Leading historian Manning Clark had insisted that, contrary to popular tradition and the view of an earlier historian, George Arnold Wood, the convicts were not the innocent victims of economic crisis but had been members of a criminal class with few redeeming qualities. Underlying these debates over the character of the convicts was, perhaps, a concern with inheritance; what did white Australia's origins as a British penal colony mean for its subsequent history and for Australians today? Two Australian historians, Lloyd Robson and A. G. L. Shaw, in separate detailed and well-researched studies, both sided with Clark rather than Wood.[16] Neither, incidentally, referred to *The Making*; their questions and concerns were quite different.

One historian of Australia's convict past who stood outside this debate on convict character and who *was* interested in the fate of the radicals and rebels transported to Australia was George Rudé, an English historian who had been in the Communist Historians Group with Eric Hobsbawm, Christopher Hill, Thompson, and others in the 1950s, and was working and living in Australia through the 1960s. Rudé was a major figure, having published a number of highly regarded essays on the social and political life of the lower classes in England and France, and the widely discussed *The Crowd in the French Revolution* in 1959.[17] Unable to find academic employment in England, it seems because of his Communist Party membership (one obituary writes of "the hundred failed job applications of the cold war years"), he took up a position at the University of Adelaide in 1960.[18] British historians saw him as having been exiled, and on at least one occasion Rudé himself referred to his own exile, declaring it to be "one of the most pleasant."[19] Once in Australia he continued to publish in England and France as before, but he also began publishing in Australia for historians of Australia. In an essay published in the Australian journal *Historical Studies* in 1963, on the topic of popular disturbances in the preindustrial age, he discussed many of the issues that Thompson addresses in *The Making*—types of disturbances, including riots, and ways to develop such studies further.[20] He urges historians not to assume there was a working class before there actually was, and to use the term "mob" more carefully than conservative historians usually did. Much of the essay is urging a detailed study of new kinds of sources, to try to discern something of the individuals who made up the crowd. He notes that the Australian records can be of great assistance here, with their enormous detail, arising from an increasingly efficient penal bureaucracy, including even the listing of the reputations of particular convicts. (A later historian has referred to the convicts sent to Australia as "among the best-documented citizens of the nineteenth-century British Empire."[21])

Rudé's essay was written before *The Making* appeared, and clearly runs in parallel with it, both texts expressing ideas developed collectively in the Communist Historians group.[22] As Harvey Kaye explains in *The British Marxist Historians,* one of the key influences on all of them was Dona Torr, who brought to the group a sense of historical passion, the view that history was "the sweat, blood, tears and triumphs of the common people, our people," and the idea that history should be written from the bottom up.[23] A later Rudé essay on the hundreds of "Captain Swing" rural protestors of 1830 who were transported to New South Wales, published in 1965, also does not refer to *The Making,* though it does refer to forthcoming unpublished research by Hobsbawm, with whom he was eventually to write a joint book on the subject.[24] Given their common background, interests, and methodological concerns, one might have expected Rudé to lead discussion in Australia on Thompson's work, but this turns out, somewhat to my surprise, not to have been the case at all, at least in print.

If *The Making* took some time to influence Australian historiography directly, the broader interest in the history of ordinary working people that had helped produce it did have an impact in the 1960s. In 1961, a group of historians led by Australian National University academics Eric Fry and Bob Gollan had formed the Australasian Society for the Study of Labour History. Along with Russel Ward, Fry had in 1956 completed one of the earliest PhDs awarded in Australia on Australian history, his work on urban wage earners in Australia in the 1880s complementing Ward's on the culture of rural workers. Gollan had encountered the Communist Historians Group when undertaking his PhD under the supervision of Harold Laski—the teacher of so many future Indian and other postcolonial national leaders—at the

London School of Economics in the late 1940s. Gollan's book, *Radical and Working Class Politics in New South Wales, 1850–1910,* based on his doctoral dissertation, had appeared the year before.[25] The society began publishing a *Bulletin* in April 1962, upgraded to a journal with its fourth issue in May 1963. Contributors saw themselves as writing a new and contentious kind of history, especially in its subject matter. Those early issues of *Labour History* included articles—academic, anecdotal, reminiscence—on issues such as strikes and riots, unions, employer-union relations, labor and radical organizations, leading labor movement figures, and radical and labor politics, parties, and ideas.

The field of Australian labor history was augmented by the appearance of Ian Turner's major work, *Industrial Labour and Politics: The Dynamics of the Labour Movement in Eastern Australia, 1900–1921* in 1965. Originally a PhD completed in 1963 and supervised by Gollan, it was a study of the changing relationships between the trade unions and labor's political organizations such as the Australian Labor Party in a period of considerable class tension, especially during World War I. It defined class as "an objective social category: the class of men and women who work for wages as distinct from the employers of labor and the self-employed," and thus embodied the idea of class as a category, or structure, that Thompson explicitly critiqued in his preface.[26] While Turner, following Marx, argued that the common interests of this class did not necessarily mean its members shared a consciousness of themselves as a class, he had not yet been influenced by Thompson's emphasis on the importance in class formation of cultural "traditions, value-systems, ideas, and institutional forms."[27]

It is not until 1967 that we begin to see Thompson influencing Australian labor historians, and then only slightly. One of the first mentions of Thompson in *Labour History* occurred that year, in the context of a symposium titled "What Is Labour History?" regarded by most subsequent commentators as inaugurating serious theoretical discussion in Australian labor history. Only two of the five contributors mentioned Thompson—Terry Irving in passing, and Eric Fry providing a longer discussion.[28] Despite the brevity of his reference to *The Making,* Irving seems to have been influenced by it, castigating Australian labor historians for assuming the existence of class antagonism. Rather, he argued, in the Australian colonies there was only a *fear* of class antagonism; the reality was that in the mid-nineteenth century there was no working class, and the "subsequent history of 'class' [in Australia] is largely a mystery."[29] A more detailed engagement came from Fry, though in his case it was with Thompson's essay, "History from Below" (published in the *Times Literary Supplement* on 7 April 1966) rather than *The Making.* Fry's contribution was interested less in the problem of how best to understand class, and more in the importance of the history of the common people. Labor history, Fry drew from Thompson, should no longer be seen as something other than, and distinct from, "proper" history, and should be understood as a diverse field, covering not only trade union histories, but also political and regional histories, and studies of "work, family, culture, religion."[30] Fry agrees with Thompson that such breadth in labor history "is not a disintegration so much as a liberation."[31]

A Rapidly Changing Historiography, 1968–1980

If Thompson's influence, especially on the understanding of class, was muted in this 1967 debate, it was to become much clearer in subsequent years. In 1968 the revised Penguin edition appeared, a cheap paperback that even students could buy. In the five years since the appearance of the first edition, a lot had happened—student rebellion, the New Left, Aboriginal protest politics, and especially growing opposition to Australia's role in the American war in Vietnam. The political center had shifted somewhat to the left, and the production of Australian history of all kinds had increased dramatically. Students began to read *The Making* for themselves. It was this revised edition that *Labour History* reviewed, having missed out on reviewing the first. The reviewer was Humphrey McQueen, a young New Left historian and trenchant critic of the Old Left, and he had mixed feelings. On the one hand, he deplored Thompson's failure to emphasize the English working class's lack of revolutionary consciousness. On the other hand, he thought that the importance of Thompson's work for the student of Australian history would be tremendous since Australia was being "made" in the years that Thompson discusses. Not only did *The Making* include important sections on the Scottish Martyrs, the Luddites, and the Cato Street Conspirators, but also and more significantly, it helped explain the total political experience Australia inherited from England and then reshaped. "Thompson," McQueen suggested, "has presented us with a valuable, if unintentional, contribution to our understanding of the ideas that many convicts and migrants brought with them."[32]

At the same time as a new generation of historians of Australia was reading and absorbing *The Making,* Rudé was continuing his exploration of the transported rebels and radicals. In a now largely forgotten but I think rather wonderful talk delivered and published in 1970, he told of his researches and the help given to him by dedicated archivists.[33] His first thought, he says, had been to look at convicts generally, but aware that Alan Shaw and Lloyd Robson were both already working on major studies, he decided to concentrate on the political prisoners. As he put it, "my real interest lay not so much in transportation as such, but rather as a projection of the social and political protest movements of the nineteenth century—primarily in Britain, but in Ireland too. So I had a dual focus: both the British and Irish and the Australian, and the interaction of the two."[34] Actually, his international focus is much wider. He describes looking for the obvious political prisoners, such as the Scottish Martyrs and the Irish rebels of the 1790s, the Cato Street conspirators, people charged with treason or sedition, the Reform Bill rioters, Chartists, Canadian rebels of the 1830s, and the Young Irishmen of 1848.[35] He then looked at social protestors transported for a variety of crimes, such as "trade unionists, machine breakers, food rioters, demolishers of turnpikes and toll gates, senders of threatening letters, and administrators of illegal oaths and at those numerous type of rebellious Irishmen such as Ribbonmen, White Boys, Oak Boys, Right Boys, Thrashers, Rockites and Lady Clares."[36] Yet again, he makes no reference to Thompson or *The Making*. I begin to wonder if there was some kind of break between the two men.

In the decade that followed, Australian historiography took off in a variety of directions, some of them influenced by *The Making*. The concern with class and politics that had been initiated by Gollan and Turner remained strong, though now historians were treating class rather differently and increasingly citing *The Making* to align themselves with a particular approach to the history of class formation. John Rickard, for example, in a 1976 study of class and politics for the period between 1890 and 1910, defined class by quoting *The Making*, to the effect that class should be defined not as a structure but something that happens.[37] Stuart Macintyre in 1978 wrote a historiographical essay titled "The Making of the Australian Working Class" whose debt to Thompson is obvious from its title.[38] He began by arguing that Thompson had redefined class for labor historians in Australia, and had dealt the vulgar Marxism that preceded him a severe blow. Australian historians, however, he went on to say, have barely begun to understand how the Australian working class was made in Thompson's sense, though all might agree it happened in the second half of the nineteenth century.

In two of the new directions that were transforming the discipline, *The Making*'s influence was more muted. In both women's history and Aboriginal history, its impact was indirect; given its focus on male rather than female working class experience and culture, and its lack of interest in empire, colonization, and questions of race, the historians creating women's and Aboriginal history had little reason to cite *The Making* directly.[39] I am not sure how many of us had actually read *The Making* in its entirety. What we often knew was the preface, with its interest in agency rather than, or at least in balance with, structure. And we knew of the term "history from below" and were taken with the idea it articulated of recovering the historical agency of powerless and hitherto invisible people.

The stimulus to women's history largely came from political engagement. For many young women historians of the 1970s, of whom I was one, the encounter with feminism, originally in the guise of Women's Liberation, transformed our politics and our approach to history. In 1970, inspired by essays in American Women's Liberation journals I had encountered as an activist, I published an article in the Left intellectual journal, *Arena*, "Historiography and Women's Liberation," setting out how I thought a focus on women's history would change the writing of Australian history generally. "The idea of women's liberation," I wrote in a way that reveals the strong connections between feminism and Marxism at this time, "is fundamental to a critique of capitalist society."[40] My historiographical references were not to Thompson or the other English Marxist historians, but to Robin Gollan, Manning Clark, and Russel Ward. In particular, I took aim, a trifle unfairly perhaps, at Ian Turner, who had written for an edited collection on Australian women a chapter titled "Prisoners in Petticoats: A Shocking History of Female Emancipation in Australia." Full of inspiration from attending Women's Liberation meetings, I castigated him roundly for failing to grasp "the very profound relationship between the social roles expected of women, the kind of economy being set up in Australia, and the development of liberal-democratic traditions," and for not stressing "the importance of the family as a fundamental unit of social organization, cutting across, but nevertheless very much affected by class."[41]

In the first issue of a scholarly journal we established in 1973, which we called *Refractory Girl*, taking our title from a ditty by convict women discovered by Anne Summers ("Factory girls, refractory girls"), our editorial excitedly declared: "We have so much to do, and it has all to be done simultaneously."[42] Five years later, in 1975, the publication of three major books demonstrated the impact of feminism on Australian history—Anne Summers's landmark work *Damned Whores and God's Police*, Edna Ryan and Anne Conlon's *Gentle Invaders: Australian Women at Work 1788–1974* and Beverley Kingston's *My Wife, My Daughter, and Poor Mary Ann*. Miriam Dixon's *The Real Matilda* followed in 1976. Together these books moved Australian feminist history from its early phase of raising questions and issuing manifestos to establishing a new field.[43] Of these four foundational texts, only *Damned Whores and God's Police* makes any reference to *The Making*, and that only in passing.[44]

Histories of Aboriginal-settler relations, colonization, and dispossession similarly did not owe a great deal to Thompson, and for the same reason—in this case, the empire and colonization had not been one of his concerns. As Robert Gregg and Madhavi Kale and others have since pointed out, Thompson's work more or less ignored empire and colonialism, with serious consequences for a time for Angophone social history.[45] Rather, these new histories were influenced either by contact with Aboriginal activists or with scholars in other disciplines, such as anthropology, who had themselves been influenced by their encounters with Aboriginal people. (Later, in the 1990s, Aboriginal people were becoming historians themselves.) These histories were beginning to make their mark in the 1970s, and were especially transformational in the 1980s. The turning point was Charles Rowley's 1970 book, *The Destruction of Aboriginal Society*; its strong emphasis on government policies and attention to dispossession, institutionalized racism, and economic exploitation helped provide a sound chronological and analytical structure for the histories which followed. By the mid-1970s a younger generation of historians was emerging, influenced by the New Left, motivated by a strong critique of racism, and often sharing a Marxist emphasis on the destructiveness of capitalism in a colonial context.[46] A new journal, *Aboriginal History,* was established at the Australian National University in 1977. In 1978, I coedited with Andrew Markus a special issue of *Labour History* on the theme of racism and the working class, which explored not only Aboriginal history but also the history and class nature of opposition to the immigration of Chinese and other nonwhite peoples.[47] Yet the connection between labor history and Aboriginal history was in fact quite weak; after two essays on Aboriginal history in this special issue, it was to be another ten years before another appeared.[48] While many labor historians had a general sympathy with Aboriginal demands for cultural respect, recognition of their prior claim to the land, and equal treatment, most had difficulty in recognizing that Aboriginal dispossession and exploitation, on the one hand, and popular support for racially based immigration policies, on the other, had profound implications for their understanding of class relations in Australia.[49]

By the second half of the 1970s, *The Making* was influential less in feminist and Aboriginal history than in their close relation, the broader and less politically inspired field of social history. As Susan Magarey explained in a helpful survey for Australian readers in *Labour History* in 1976 of the new social history in Britain, social history was becoming securely established. Thompson himself had established a Centre for the Study of Social History at the University of Warwick in 1968, and two new journals—*Social History* and *History Workshop Journal*—had just appeared. Australians working on British history were inspired by this new British social history, and their enthusiasm soon spread to those studying Australian history. Its influence was evident first in convict history. Rudé's book, *Protest and Punishment: The Story of the Social and Political Protestors Transported to Australia, 1788–1868,* appeared in 1978. Though clearly working in the same tradition as Thompson, with its emphasis on the ideas and experiences of British radical protesters, it actually made no direct reference to *The Making,* although it did cite *Whigs and Hunters* in the context of discussing the difficulty of distinguishing between "social" crimes and crimes of theft. Australian historians did not receive *Protest and Punishment* well; their principal critique was that its research was so detailed that Rudé could no longer see the wood for the trees.[50] Yet revisiting the book recently, I am struck by the depth and originality of its research, and the success at one level at least of its transnational enterprise. In following the political prisoners as he did, and seeking to understand their experiences and identity as they were so abruptly transplanted from one society to another, Rudé, it seems to me now, is engaging in just the kind of imperial, settler colonial, and transnational history that many of us so seek to undertake today. Where Thompson remained resolutely focused on England, with short excursions to Scotland, Wales, and Ireland, Rudé's intellectual interests traveled freely between Britain, France, and the British colonies.

In any case, if Australian historians were lukewarm toward Rudé's *Protest and Punishment,* Thompson himself was downright hostile and acerbic. In a review in *New Society* in December 1978, he wrote "the book disappoints. It is even quite bad."[51] His argument is essentially that Rudé, working in Australia on Australian archives, had lost touch with the best work happening in Britain, being seemingly unaware of some recent doctoral theses and other work. Thompson denigrates Rudé's extensive and original Tasmanian research, saying "Rudé has absolute faith in the original and prior virtue of scraps of Tasmanian prison archives over all other sources." The burden of the review is that you can do better Australian history in England than in Australia. There is no need, he says, for further research on how the protesters experienced life as convicts in the colonies, as we know all we need to know from Joyce Marlow (referring presumably to her book on the Tolpuddle Martyrs), though it would be useful, he says, to know more about how they lived once released from servitude. These criticisms strike me as profoundly unfair, and they helped to bury an important if only partially successful book. Sadly, they are consistent with the experiences of those Australian historians who sought to meet or work with Thompson during the 1970s. They all report that he, like Hobsbawm but not others of that generation such as John Saville and Royden Harrison, was profoundly uninterested in, and dismissive of, Australian history and historiography, seeing it has having no relevance to his own work and of little interest or significance for others.

Yet if Thompson did not value Australian history and those who sought to understand it better, Australian historians, especially of the convict era, were increasingly warming to him. Alan Atkinson's 1979 essay, "Four Patterns of Convict Protest," in which he saw two classes—the masters and the convicts—in formation, approvingly quotes *The Making*'s preface to say, "Class is defined by men as they live their own history, and, in the end, this is the only definition." Alan, who went on to become a leading exponent of Australian social history, tells me he probably bought the book in 1977, and that he cannot think of any other writer who influenced him more. "Four Patterns of Protest," he wrote to me in an email, depended essentially on Thompson.[52] The essay argues that in the 1820s in New South Wales we see two social classes—masters and convicts—born in a legal and economic relationship to one another. It stresses that what convicts believed to be right and fair arose from a "system of unequal relationships," in which the masters held most of the power and the magistrates helped them retain it.[53] Through a process of dialogue between masters and convicts, emerged a fragile set of assumptions about rights; convicts internalized the rules of conduct, and took action when they thought the rules had been broken.[54] Atkinson's achievement was to break from the tradition of scholarship debating the moral character of the convicts and to replace it with a new kind of convict history grounded in an analysis of changing class relationships in a specific legal and economic context.

Despite the strong connections between social and labor history, the leading Australian proponents of the new Thompsonian social history were connected less to labor history than to the ethno-historical endeavors of Australian historians working in other fields, such as Rhys Isaacs on colonial America and Inga Clendinnen on the Aztecs. The interest was primarily in how to discover the perspectives of those who left few records of their own. In 1979, Inga Clendinnen's essay, "Understanding the Heathen at Home: E. P. Thompson and His School," published in *Historical Studies*, drew these strands together for an Australian audience. For her the exciting thing was Thompson's ability to deduce from action the nature of culture and consciousness, or systems of "shared expectation and meanings."[55] She praised Thompson for rescuing the study of English political culture from "the twin banalities of complacent Whigs and reductionist Marxists."[56] It was around this time that Greg Dening, a leading ethno-historian based at the University of Melbourne, polled academic staff there asking them to name the most influential work of history for them; Thompson's work topped the charts.[57]

The Peak of Influence

It was in the 1980s and early 1990s that Thompson's impact was most strongly felt, in a range of fields—class theory and history, the study of popular culture, and, eventually, Aboriginal history. The decade opened with Bob Connell and Terry Irving' major book, *Class Structure in Australian History*, published in 1980, which served as something of a key text in Australian labor and class history in the 1980s. Its debt to Thompson, however, is uneven. On the one hand, it discusses his work warmly, quoting his paragraphs on class as something that happens, as an historical relationship, and as a product of human agency. On the other hand, it seeks to retain a notion of class structure, as its title clearly indicates, and to integrate Thompsonian notions of fluidity with structuralism's sense of "the intractability of class relations."[58] The result is awkward, complicated perhaps by a difficulty in coming to terms with the new scholarship on gender and race. While *Class Structure in Australian History* pays some attention to gender, it pays little to race, and neither issue forms a significant part of its argument about class.

More explicit debts were articulated at around this time in the growing field of cultural history. An essay collection edited by Susan Dermody, John Docker, and Drusilla Modjeska called *Nellie Melba, Ginger Meggs, and Friends: Essays in Australian Cultural History*, begins with an extensive discussion of the emerging Australian cultural studies. These scholars were deeply interested in the work of Stuart Hall and the Birmingham Centre for Cultural Studies, and saw Thompson as a key figure in the emergence of a new form of cultural theory.[59] Thompson's emphasis on working class radical and popular movements, the editors suggest in their introduction, worked both against "official Marxism with its perceived narrow focus on the economic" and against the Cold War "end of ideology" thesis that the working class, now prosperous, was apathetic, without culture.[60] Two years later, John Docker in *In a Critical Condition* drew attention to the challenge Thompson, with his emphasis first in *William Morris* (1955) and then *The Making* on "popular, radical and artisan cultures," presented to established narrow textualist and metaphysical approaches in literary criticism such as Leavisism and New Criticism.[61]

Some of the key figures in the Indian subaltern studies project were working in Australia in the 1980s, notably Ranajit Guha and Dipesh Chakrabarty. Guha, founder of the subaltern studies group, had arrived at the Australian National University as a senior research fellow in 1980; from there he edited the influential first volume of *Subaltern Studies*, which appeared in 1982. Chakrabarty was there at the same time, completing his ANU PhD dissertation on the jute workers of Calcutta 1890–1940 the following year. The group sought to develop a new kind of Indian history, to go beyond existing approaches that focused on imperial and nationalist elites, and to rework anew for India the idea of history from below. Like Thompson and the other Marxist historians, they wanted to rescue Indian socially subordinate groups, especially the peasantry, from "the condescension of posterity" and to make them present in their own history.[62] As the project went on, its practitioners were increasingly attracted to post-structuralist critiques of Thompsonian notions of consciousness and experience, and to poststructuralist methods for reading and deconstructing colonial texts.[63]

This work came to influence those working in Australian history, especially Aboriginal history, but the connections were not as soon or as great as one might expect. None of the key works in Aboriginal history of the 1980s—Henry Reynolds's *The Other Side of the Frontier* (1981) and *Frontier* (1987), Ann McGrath's *Born in the Cattle* (1987), and Bain Attwood's *The Making of the Aborigines* (1989)—refer to it or show signs of being influenced by it, though their interest in subaltern perspectives and cultural practices in a colonial situation was similar.[64] A significant point of contact, however, came a little later, in 1991, with Dipesh Chakrabarty's article, "Postcoloniality and the Artifice of History," which challenged historians generally to consider why it was that Indian historians had to engage closely with European historiography, while those working in European historiographical fields did not feel obliged to reciprocate. "Whether it is an Edward Thompson, a Le Roy Ladurie, a George Duby, a Carlo Ginzberg," he wrote, "the 'greats' and the models of the historian's enterprise are always at least culturally 'European'."[65] The article, perhaps, resonated with Australian historians' sense, in their studies of settler colonialism, of their complicated relation to European historiographical tradition, and challenged them to rethink the ways they understood empire and colonialism in relation to their own historiographical enterprise.

While Australian Aboriginal history as a field was not especially indebted either to Thompson directly or to subaltern studies' readings of him, one historian at around this time did make a serious attempt to apply Thompson's method and insights to Aboriginal history. In *The Making of the*

Aborigines, Bain Attwood set out to write an Australian Aboriginal history on the model of *The Making.* He wanted, he writes in the introduction, to understand how the diverse and numerous Indigenous groups in Australia came to be seen, and saw themselves, as a single people called "Aborigines," subject to cultural forms of domination.[66] His debt to Thompson is overt in its attempt to analyze the making of the Aborigines "in terms similar to E. P. Thompson's study of the English working class."[67] Attwood criticizes historians for hitherto stressing either only European or only Aboriginal agency and autonomy, and says he seeks to understand "the complex interdependence of structure and agency."[68] Above all, he says, he sought to transpose Thompson's understanding of class as a social and cultural formation into the Australian context by replacing "class" with "Aborigines."[69] Near the end of the book he says Aboriginal people "made themselves as well as being made."[70] And the book deals with Aboriginal perspectives and experience, though the weight of the analysis tends to lie more with the colonizers than the colonized.

Social history of a Thompsonian kind, meanwhile, was taking hold. The labor historians were so enamored by the idea of "history from below" and the social history that flowed from it that in 1981 the journal *Labour History* adopted a subtitle—*A Journal of Labour and Social History.* By the second half of the decade, labor historians were borrowing their titles from *The Making*—two examples are John Merritt's *The Making of the AWU* (1986), and Ray Markey's *The Making of the Labor Party in New South Wales 1880–1900* (1988).[71] Yet curiously, neither drew on Thompson to develop their argument. In their borrowing from his title, they were nevertheless paying tribute to Thompson, as historians around this time were doing around the world.[72]

Closer, perhaps, to Thompson's project was *Australians: An Historical Library,* a set of ten volumes prepared as the contribution from professional historians to the 1988 bicentennial commemorations. These volumes, products of the first major university-based exercise in collaborative work in Australian history on a national scale, provided hitherto undreamt-of opportunities to exchange ideas and learn new methods. The instigator of the project, Australian social historian Ken Inglis, decided to organize the volumes on the "slice" principle, by including along with several reference volumes five narrative volumes designated for the periods and years of 1788, 1838, 1888, 1938, and 1988. The three middle volumes, focusing as they did on a single year, offered an excellent opportunity to develop some of the methods and approaches of the new social history. For many of the historians attracted to the project, here was an opportunity to write social history as a mix of Thompson's "history from below" and ethno-history, capturing multiple perspectives and understandings.[73]

Two of the historians attracted to the project were Alan Atkinson and Marian Aveling, who became the editors of the 1838 volume. Atkinson brought an interest in convict culture and class relations strongly influenced by *The Making,* while Aveling brought preoccupations derived from the growing field of feminist history, with its interest in gender relations, sexuality, and family life. Their collaboration brought feminist history closer to social history than otherwise might have occurred; given *The Making*'s own relative silence on female working class experience and culture, it was rarely referred to or quoted in Australian feminist historical texts at this time.[74] Not only did the 1838 volume exemplify the new social history, but also Alan Atkinson the following year published *Camden*, a detailed study of a community south of Sydney involving masters and their convict, ex-convict, and free laborers in the period from approximately 1820 to 1850. It, too, with its theme that in a small community we can see how one social order can be swept aside by another, was strongly influenced by Thompson.[75]

By the 1990s, it had become commonplace to cite *The Making* and to assert how much it had changed the way we do history. If we are to be precise, though, it was not *The Making* as a book but its short and pithy preface that everyone now knew. With the decline in teaching and research in British history from its heyday in the 1960s as other histories—American, Australian, Asian, Continental European, world—grew in popularity, students were just as likely to encounter *The Making* in courses on these other histories, or on theory and method, as on specifically British history. The result was that it was the preface, with its central idea of ordinary people being present at their own history, and its warning against the condescension of posterity, that they now most likely knew. As one friend who was a student at the University of Sydney in the 1990s wrote to me, "I read the Preface in a first year European history course, and I think every year thereafter, and eventually the whole book." Another, a student also in the 1990s, put it the other way around: "I read most of it [the book] and the Preface many times then and since."[76]

Whether we are talking of the preface or the book as a whole, *The Making* was foundational for the development of cultural history in Australia as elsewhere, involving a different set of historians from those in labor history. Indeed, because cultural history incorporated not only a Thompsonian interest in class and history from below but also a poststructuralist interest in representation, language, and textuality, labor historians tended to maintain their distance. In 1994, I criticized them for doing so, using as my starting point the American historian Lynn Hunt's edited collection of essays, *The New Cultural History*.[77] In one of my few discussions of *The Making* in print, I suggested that the kind of history the cultural historians were developing owed a lot to Thompson. In *The Making*, he had, I wrote, "rescued the British Marxist historical tradition from its dry determinism, its historicism, its teleology, and its concern only with broad structures and with a very limited form of economic history. In stressing class as a relationship that emerges at a particular time in a specific context, he gave the Marxist tradition new life. ... It was, above all, class as a culturally specific phenomenon that interested him. It is this aspect of Marxism that flourishes best today, and which gives labor history some of its continuing vitality."[78]

The problem, I thought, was that even though labor historians, through Thompson especially, had themselves been present at the making of cultural history, they now stood apart. I urged them to give up their continuing attachment to Marxist structuralism, with its distinction between underlying or hidden structures and the surface reality we see and experience. The poststructuralist critique of structuralism should be welcomed, I urged, for in some ways it was liberating. Instead of having to find and fix the "real" meaning of any event, period, or practice, historians could instead explore a diversity of meanings and perspectives, and their complexity and interrelationships. I suggested that for historians, structuralism was "a confining straitjacket, a closing of possibilities, an illusory end to the analytical rainbow."[79]

Cultural history has since flourished in Australia, though not so much in labor history, despite the urgings of people like me and another Australian historian, Frank Bongiorno.[80] Perhaps for labor historians the problem was that cultural history, like historiography more generally, was losing interest in class. With its interest in the multiple sources whereby some groups become marginal, excluded, dominated, and exploited by others, cultural history gave class relatively less importance than labor historians wished to do. By the mid-1990s, it was the cultural rather than the labor historians who continued to acknowledge the influence of Thompson, as Richard Waterhouse did in his history of Australian popular culture in 1995.[81] In their edited collection, *Cultural History in Australia*, Hsu-Ming Teo and Richard White asserted that there was little doubt that *The Making* had made the greatest impact on Anglophone social and cultural history. He had, they said, pioneered the process of writing "history from below," to see how workers made cultural sense of their experience and created collective political identities.[82]

New Histories in the New Century

By the 2000s, the influence of *The Making* had become largely indirect, embedded as it was in the now established fields of social and cultural history. The rate of citation, discussion, and acknowledgement of influence slowed. Furthermore, interest in the British imperial context of Australian history had returned, enlivened by feminist and postcolonial approaches shared with scholars in Britain and the United States. One aspect of this interest has been a revolution in convict history in the last twenty years, in the work of Cassandra Pybus, Hamish Maxwell-Stuart, and Emma Christopher, among others, that has placed convict history within a global history of unfree labor migration in which histories of slavery, indentured labor, incarceration, and colonization were intertwined through imperial and post-imperial trading networks.[83] In this context, *The Making of the English Working Class* remains a paradox: it is a local and national history whose central ideas have crossed international borders and been reworked in curious and wonderful ways. It is not the only book—not by a long shot—to have stressed agency, culture, reading sources against the grain, and respecting one's historical subjects, but it did these things in a way that inspired and made sense to several generations of humanities scholars around the world, including in Australia.

Curiously, hardly anyone in Australia in 2013 thought to organize a symposium or other event to mark the fiftieth anniversary of the publication of *The Making*, as happened in the United States, Canada, the UK, and elsewhere.[84] Perhaps we have become so engaged in new questions that *The Making* has receded in importance for us, or perhaps—and this is my preferred view—we have absorbed its lessons so well that we have forgotten where we learnt them.

***Ann Curthoys** writes about class, race, gender, and colonialism in Australian history as well as reflections on the nature of historical writing. She is the author of* Freedom Ride: A Freedom Rider Remembers *(2002); co-author with John Docker of* Is History Fiction? *(2010); co-author with Jessie Mitchell of* Taking Liberty: Indigenous Rights and Settler Self-Government in Colonial Australia, 1830–1890 *(2018), and is writing a book on Paul and Eslanda Robeson's tour of Australia and New Zealand in 1960. She is professor emerita at the Australian National University and an honorary professor at the University of Sydney.*

Notes

I wish to thank Catie Gilchrist, John Docker, Penny Russell, Chips Sowerwine, Stuart Macintyre, Terry Irving, Ken Macnab, George Parsons, and the Australian Research Council for their assistance.

1. See, for example, John Docker, *In a Critical Condition* (Melbourne: Penguin, 1984), esp. 49–63.
2. My thanks to Ken Macnab for copies of his reading lists and lecture notes.
3. Sue Bellamy, comment to Ann Curthoys on Facebook, 27 October 2013.
4. Robert Barrie Rose, "Eighteenth-Century Price Riots and Public Policy," *International Review of Social History* 6, no. 2 (1961): 277–292. See also George Parsons, "Clio's Language War: Ancient and Modern Historians at Macquarie University in the 1970s," *History Australia* 5, no. 3 (2008): 79n1. Parsons writes: "Professor R. B. Rose, the historian of the popular movements in eighteenth century Britain and France, had suffered during the McCarthyist period in English academia in the 1950s and 1960s."
5. For a much more extended discussion, see Ann Curthoys, "We've Just Started Making National Histories and You Want Us to Stop Already?" in *After the Imperial Turn: Thinking with and through the Nation*, ed. Antoinette Burton (Durham, NC: Duke University Press, 2003), 70–89. See also Mark McKenna, *An Eye for Eternity: The Life of Manning Clark* (Melbourne: Melbourne University Press, 2011).
6. The similarity is noticed in the introduction to Hsu-Ming Teo and Richard White, eds., *Cultural History in Australia* (Sydney: University of New South Wales Press, 2003), 16.

7. Russel Ward completed a Master's thesis on modernist poetry in 1949: R. B. Ward, "The Genesis and Nature of the Social, Political and Historical Content of English Poetry between the Two World Wars, with Particular Reference to the Works of Pound, Eliot and Auden" (MA thesis, University of Adelaide, 1949).
8. See John Docker, *In a Critical Condition* (Melbourne: Penguin, 1984), 36–37.
9. See Hugh Anderson, "Man on a Bough: Dedication and Tribute. [To Russel Braddock Ward]," *Australian Folklore* 9, (1994): xi–xiii.
10. Jeremy Beckett, untitled memoir, *Journal of Australian Colonial History* (hereafter JACH) 10, no. 2 (2008): 10–11.
11. See Frank Bongiorno and David Andrew Roberts, "Introduction" *JACH* 10, no. 2 (2008): vii.
12. David Kent, untitled memoir, *JACH* 10, no. 2 (2008): 8.
13. Ibid., 9.
14. George Parsons, "The Cato Street Conspirators in New South Wales," *Labour History* 8 (1965): 1.
15. Email Parsons to Ann Curthoys, 25 October 2013.
16. A. G. Shaw, *Convicts and the Colonies: A Study of Penal Transportation from Great Britain and Ireland to Australia* (London: Faber, 1966); Lloyd Robson, *The Convict Settlers of Australia* (Melbourne: Melbourne University Press, 1994). See David Andrew Roberts, "Russel Ward and the Convict Legend," *JACH* 10, no. 2 (2008): 37–58.
17. See James Friguglietti, "A Scholar in Exile: George Rudé as a Historian of Australia," in *French History and Civilization: Papers from the George Rudé Seminar,* vol. 1 (Melbourne: Victoria, 12005), 3–12.
18. Hugh Stretton, "George Frederick Elliot Rude," Obituary in *Proceedings of the Australian Academy of the Humanities* 18 (1993): 64–66.
19. Friguglietti, "A Scholar in Exile," 4.
20. George Rude, "The Study of Popular Disturbances in the 'Pre-Industrial' Age," *Historical Studies: Australia and New Zealand* 10, no. 40 (1963): 457–469.
21. Norma Townsend, "Reconstructed Lives: The Swing Transportees in New South Wales" *Australian Studies* 16, no. 2 (2001): 20.
22. For discussion of E. P. Thompson and his marginal connection to the Communist Historians Group, see John Saville, *Memoirs from the Left* (London: Merlin Press, 2003), 104.
23. Harvey Kaye, *The British Marxist Historians* (Cambridge: Polity Press, 1984), 14, quoting Saville et al. in the foreword to *Democracy and the Labor Movement*, 8.
24. George Rude, "'Captain Swing' in New South Wales," *Historical Studies: Australia and New Zealand* 12, no. 44 (1965): 467–480; Eric Hobsbawm and George Rude, *Captain Swing: A Social History of the Great English Agricultural Uprising of 1830* (New York: Norton, [1968] 1975).
25. R. A. Gollan, "Radicalism and Socialism in Eastern Australia, 1850–1910: A Study in Political Ideas in Relation to Economic Development" (PhD diss., LSE, 1951).
26. Ian Turner, *Industrial Labor and Politics: the Dynamics of the Labor Movement in Eastern Australia, 1900–1921* (Canberra: ANU Press, 1965), xiv. See critique from Stuart Macintyre, "The Making of the Australian Working Class: An Historiographical Survey," *Historical Studies: Australia and New Zealand* 18, no. 71 (1978): esp. 243. Turner later accepted the force of Macintyre's criticism in his new introduction to the 1979 edition, available at http://members.optushome.com.au/spainter/Indlabor.html.

27. E. P. Thompson, *The Making of the English Working Class* (Harmondsworth: Penguin, 1968), 10.
28. E. C. Fry et al., "Symposium: What Is Labour History?" *Labour History* 12 (1967): 60–81.
29. T. H. Irving, contribution to ibid, 80–81.
30. Eric Fry, contribution to ibid, 62–63.
31. Ibid., 63.
32. Humphrey McQueen, review of E. P. Thompson, *The Making of the English Working Class,* 2nd ed., 1968, in *Labour History* 15 (1969): 75–77.
33. George Rudé, "The Archivist and the Historian," *Papers and Proceedings of the Tasmanian Historical Research Association* 17, no. 4 (1970): 111–128.
34. Ibid., 113–114.
35. Ibid., 114.
36. Ibid., 115.
37. John Rickard, *Class and Politics: New South Wales, Victoria, and the Early Commonwealth, 1890–1910* (Canberra: ANU Press, 1976).
38. Macintyre, "The Making of the Australian Working Class."
39. For a forceful exposition of these criticisms of *The Making,* see Robert Gregg and Madhavi Kale, "The Empire and Mr Thompson: Making of Indian Princes and English Working Class," *Economic and Political Weekly* 32, no. 36 (September 1997): 2273–2288.
40. Ann Curthoys, "Historiography and Women's Liberation," *Arena* 22 (1970): 35.
41. Curthoys, "Historiography and Women's Liberation," 39.
42. *Refractory Girl* 1 (1973): 1.
43. See Ann Curthoys, "Visions, Nightmares, Dreams: Women's History, 1975," *Australian Historical Studies* 27, no. 106 (1996): 1–13.
44. Anne Summers, *Damned Whores and God's Police: The Colonization of Women in Australia* (Melbourne: Penguin, 1975), 169. Miriam Dixson used another Thompson work, *Customs in Common,* to argue that Australian culture had powerfully rebellious strain inherited from eighteenth century England. See Miriam Dixson, *The Real Matilda*: *Woman and Identity in Australia, 1788 to the Present* (Melbourne: Penguin, 1976), 271.
45. Gregg and Kale, "The Empire and Mr Thompson."
46. One notable example was Raymond Evans, Kay Saunders, and Kathryn Cronin, *Exclusion, Exploitation and Extermination: Race Relations in Colonial Queensland* (Brisbane: University of Queensland Press, 1975).
47. Ann Curthoys and Andrew Markus, eds., *Who Are Our Enemies? Racism and the Working Class in Australia* (Sydney: Hale and Iremonger, 1978).
48. See Rae Frances, Ann McGrath, and Bruce Scates, "Broken Silences? *Labour History* and Aboriginal workers," in *Challenges to Labour History,* ed. Terry Irving (Sydney: UNSW Press, 1994), 189–211.
49. Ann Curthoys, "An Historiographical Paradox: Brian Fitzpatrick, the British Empire, and Indigenous Histories," in *Brian Fitzpatrick and Manning Clark,* ed. Stuart Macintyre and Sheila Fitzpatrick (Melbourne: Melbourne University Press, 2007), 70–87; see also Gregg and Kale, "The Empire and Mr Thompson."
50. See reviews by A. T. Yarwood in *Australian Journal of Politics and History* 26, no. 1 (1980): 141–142; Eric Richards in *Historical Studies* 19, no. 74 (1980): 1401; David Phillips in *The English Historical Review* 95, no. 375 (1980): 375–377. More laudatory is A. W. Stargardt's review in *Public Affairs* 52, no. 3 (1979): 560–561.

51. E. P. Thompson, "Sold Like a Sheep for a Pound," *New Society* 14 (December 1978), reprinted in E. P. Thompson, *Making History: Writings on History and Culture* (New York: New Press, 1994), 191–199, quote on 192.
52. Alan Atkinson to Ann Curthoys, email 8 January 2014.
53. Alan Atkinson, "Four Patterns of Convict Protest," *Labour History* 37 (1979): 35, 43.
54. Ibid., 43.
55. Inga Clendinnen, "Understanding the Heathen at Home: E. P. Thompson and His School," *Historical Studies: Australia and New Zealand* 18, no. 72 (1979): 436. Her interest was not so much in *The Making* as in Thompson's subsequent essays, notably "The Moral Economy of the English Crowd in the Eighteenth Century."
56. Ibid., 439.
57. Personal communication from Chips Sowerwine, email, 29 May 2013.
58. R. W. Connell and T. H. Irving, *Class Structure in Australian History: Documents, Narrative and Argument* (Melbourne: Longman Cheshire, 1980), 11.
59. Susan Dermody, John Docker, and Drusilla Modjeska, eds., *Nellie Melba, Ginger Meggs, and Friends: essays in Australian Cultural History* (Malmsbury, Victoria: Kibble Books, 1982), 1–8.
60. Ibid., 1.
61. Docker, *In a Critical Condition*, 49–50.
62. Dipesh Chakrabarty, "Subaltern Studies and Postcolonial Historiography," *Neplanta: Views from South* 1, no. 1 (2000): 14–15.
63. Ibid., 24.
64. Henry Reynolds, *The Other Side of the Frontier: An Interpretation of the Aboriginal Response to the Invasion and Settlement of Australia* (Townsville: History Department, James Cook University, 1981); Ann McGrath, *Born in the Cattle: Aborigines in Cattle Country* (Sydney: Allen and Unwin, 1987); Bain Attwood, *The Making of the Aborigines* (Sydney: Allen and Unwin, 1989).
65. Dipesh Chakrabarty, "Postcoloniality and the Artifice of History: Who Speaks for 'Indian' Pasts?" *Representations* 37 (1992): 1–26, quote on 2.
66. Bain Attwood, *The Making of the Aborigines* (Sydney: Allen and Unwin, 1987), x.
67. Ibid., xii.
68. Ibid., 147.
69. Ibid., 149.
70. Ibid., 150.
71. John Merritt, *The Making of the AWU* (Melbourne: Oxford University Press, 1986); Ray Markey, *The Making of the Labor Party in New South Wales, 1880–1900* (Sydney: University of New South Wales Press, 1988).
72. See Dipesh Chakrabarty, "The Lost Causes of E. P. Thompson," *Labour/Le Travail* 72 (2013): 207.
73. Marian Aveling, "My Life in History," *History Australia* 10, no. 3 (2013): 258–259.
74. There were stray examples, such as Elizabeth Windschuttle, "Discipline, Domestic Training and Social Control: The Female School of Industry, Sydney, 1826–1847," *Labour History* 39 (1980): 1–14 and Judith Smart, "Feminists, Food and the Fair Prices: The Cost of Living Demonstrations in Melbourne, August–September 1917," *Labour History* 50 (1986): 113–131, esp. 115–117.
75. Alan Atkinson, *Camden: Farm and Village Life in Early New South Wales* (Melbourne: Oxford University Press, 1988). See Atkinson's own discussion of this book in Alan Atkinson, "History in the Academy," in *Australian History Now*, ed. Anna Clark and Paul Ashton (Sydney: New South Books, 2013), 114.

76. Zora Simic and Marina Bollinger, comments to Ann Curthoys on Facebook, 27 October 2013.
77. Lynn Hunt, *The New Cultural History* (Berkeley: University of California Press, 1989).
78. Ann Curthoys, "Labour History and Cultural Studies," *Labour History,* no. 67 (1994): 12–21.
79. Ibid., 21.
80. Frank Bongiorno, "Class, Populism and Labour Politics in Victoria, 1890–1914," *Labour History* 66 (1994): 14–32.
81. Richard Waterhouse, *Private Pleasures, Public Leisure: A History of Australian Popular Culture since 1788* (Melbourne: Longman, 1995), x.
82. Hsu-ming Teo and Richard White, eds., *Cultural History in Australia* (Sydney: University of New South Wales Press, 2003), 8.
83. See Emma Christopher and Hamish Maxwell-Stewart, "Convict Transportation in Global Context, c. 1700–88," in *The New Cambridge History of Australia,* vol. 1, ed. Alison Bashford and Stuart Macintyre (Cambridge: Cambridge University Press, 2013), 68–90.
84. The only commemoration I am aware of was by a group called Historical Materialism Australasia, which chose for its 2013 annual conference theme "Making and Unmaking Class." The call for papers read: "On the 50th anniversary of the publication of E. P. Thompson's epochal *The Making of the English Working Class,* we are seeking to question again how class is made (and unmade), and to do so in the spirit Thompson exemplified: with an allergy to cant and an abhorrence of received ideas." The conference included papers on *The Making,* and on related topics. For more information, visit http://philevents.org/event/show/9476 and at http://hmaustralasia.files.wordpress.com/2013/02/hm-australasia-program.pdf, both accessed on 22 September 2014.

Chapter 3

The Ecology of Class

Revolution, Weaponized Nature, and the Making of Campesino *Consciousness*

Christopher R. Boyer

The chapter at the dead center of *The Making of the English Working Class* is simply titled "Community." Like much of the book, it casts a romantic eye over England's agrarian past as it narrates how industrialization transformed the rural landscape into an industrialized space that "destroyed the balance between rural and urban life."[1] As villagers took jobs in Lancashire mills or migrated from Ireland to the docks of Liverpool and the factories of Manchester, Thompson argues that they did not so much forget their traditions as lose the leisure time to indulge them. The commodification of labor and natural resources, along with the progressive immiseration of the countryside, Thompson argued, reordered the sinews of social solidarity. Eventually, the bonds of village life faded as memories of sowing and reaping, sports, and community festivals withered away. In Thompson's telling, these rich touchstones of identity inexorably gave way to one central element of social cohesion: "[T]hat which the working people, in antagonism of their labour and to their masters, built for themselves."[2] The dialectical process of creating such a sense of "felt cohesion" is of course the story that Thompson relates about the formation of class in the England of the industrial revolution.

Thompson might have overstated the extent to which class identity supplanted rural people's identification with their places of origin. In Mexico, for example, at least some industrial workers tended to divide along the lines of geographic origin and turn against each other, rather than developing a shared antagonism to their "masters," as Thompson put it.[3] Yet there can be no question that rural Mexicans experienced some of what Thompson's idealized English country people did. Mexican villagers left home to take work in the cities or, more commonly, rural industries such as railroads, mines, sawmills, and textile factories. Even those who remained behind faced an increasingly industrialized landscape in some regions, as the great rural estates known as haciendas acquired the attributes of agribusinesses. Lazy cattle farms in the northwestern Yucatán became henequen haciendas that produced raw material for International Harvester. Growing demand for sugar spurred estates in the center-south state of Morelos to adopt an industrial model of sugar production and eventually helped spark the agrarian revolution headed by Emiliano Zapata. The late nineteenth-century transportation revolution created new markets for rice from the coasts, cotton from the northern Laguna district, timber from the highlands, and coffee from the southern mountains. It also commodified the land and encouraged speculation in agricultural property, potential mining sites, and other natural resources. New laws (or new interpretations of old ones) privatized the commons nearly everywhere, opening the way for outsiders and wealthier residents to acquire land. The scale of dispossession and commodification was one factor among many that sparked the 1910–1915 revolution.[4]

The dispossession of the nineteenth century and social upheaval of the early twentieth established the social backdrop for a postrevolutionary agrarian movement in the 1920s that redefined peasants as members of a class-like social category known as *el campesinado,* or more commonly as *campesinos.* Nowadays, poor rural people who either own their own small parcels or who work as rural laborers are nearly universally called *campesinos* in Mexico and throughout Latin America. However, the term itself—and more important, the implicit concept of class that it conveys—was rarely used before the 1910 revolution. As I have argued elsewhere, rural people usually were identified solely through their villages or origin or perhaps as the ethnically inflected members of (putatively indigenous) *pueblos* before the revolution. They only "became" *campesinos* in the postrevolutionary decades. This transition took place as increasing numbers of rural people took advantage of the land reform in the 1920s and early 1930s and came to rhetorically embrace a common history of "oppression" at the hands of landowners. Not all rural people "became" *campesinos* in this sense, but those who did tended to acknowledge that they shared a common set of politico-economic "interests" in land reform and "enemies" in the form of landowners and other so-called counterrevolutionaries. This cycle of dispossession, revolution, and land reform formed the cohesive bonds that made Mexican *campesinos* into a social category that, at least rhetorically, functioned as a peasant class.[5]

Landowners did not passively forfeit their social status and property to uppity rural people. Some turned to friends in high places in a bid to have their property exempted from redistribution. Others organized private militias known as "white guards" to intimidate villagers and encourage them not to request land reform parcels. Generations have recognized these well-worn strategies.[6] Yet many landowners also employed a more passive strategy that involved sabotaging territory slated for redistribution. Some dammed up creeks or irrigation canals that customarily flowed to cornfields that *campesinos* now claimed as their own; others clear-cut forests slated for delivery to rural communities. In other words, landowners often used nature as a weapon of class contention. Their willingness to harm the land rather than deliver it to peasants brought nature into the realm of social struggle and functionally associated *campesinos* with the defense of the land's ecological integrity.[7]

Political leaders rarely made mention of these practical questions of injury to the land itself. Instead, radical governors, labor organizers, and village radicals articulated postrevolutionary tropes of historical injustice. They tended to dwell on the abstract ideas that equated land reform with social justice. Marxist variants of this postrevolutionary agrarianism depicted the land as a means of production that the agrarian reform could deliver back to its original (or at least) rightful owners. More moderate politicians eschewed the language of class struggle in favor of a less incendiary land-to-the-tiller rhetoric; they drew on liberal ideas of ownership and rights *campesinos* deserved the land that had been illegally seized from them in previous decades. Both the Marxist and liberal social justice variants of post-revolutionary ideology depicted landowners as insatiable profiteers who victimized villagers. Both versions depicted the land in generic terms not as an organic and living ecosystem but rather as medium with which to repay rural people for past injustices. *Campesinos'* right to request land, according to this postrevolutionary revolutionary logic, derived from circumstances that were both chronologically and ontologically prior to the land reform, and even to the revolution itself.[8]

Yet that is not how many rural people experienced land reform. While most villagers seem to have resented commodification and dispossession of the land, and some joined revolutionary armies to do something about it, the moral outrage that led them to turn against the hacienda regime oftentimes became solidified only after the revolution had ended, as landowners not only put up barriers to land reform but in many instances sabotaged the acreage that became slated for redistribution. The apparent willingness of the landed oligarchy to use water, forests, and perhaps fire as "weapons of the powerful" lent credence to revolutionary critiques of their inherently reactionary character. Practice and rhetoric converged as landowners, who had at one point in time depended on peasant labor to plant bring in crops, now turned squarely against *campesinos*—and in some instances entire villages—who requested land reform parcels.

The generalization and institutionalization of mutual animosity between *campesinos* and landowners broke down what Thompson defined as a moral economy that had once bound the two groups together, even if uncomfortably. In the prerevolutionary era, *campesinos* and hacienda owners depended on each other for economic survival—even in a context of mutual distrust. Land reform undermined this regime little by little and replaced what Eric Wolf described the uneasy symbiosis between landowner and peasant village with a logic of class antagonism.[9] Peasants developed a new sense of class consciousness in the Thompsonian sense of the way in which experiences "are handled in cultural terms: embodied in traditions, value systems, ideas, and institutional forms."[10] This article argues that these two processes—the violation of a moral economy and the establishment of a sense of class consciousness—were mutually supportive in postrevolutionary Mexico, a process most fully described by Thompson's discussion of community in *The Making*, in which one set of bonds (call it a prerevolutionary moral economy) is replaced by new ones built around understandings of collective interest (call it class consciousness). Understanding this process demands that we pay closer attention to the way that rural people and hacienda owners related not only to the political ideas of the era, but to nature itself.

Moreover, I argue that *campesino* consciousness in Mexico originated in response to the deliberate destruction—what I call the "weaponization"—of natural resources that became particularly prevalent during the process of land reform. This weaponization was more marked in some regions than others; agrarianism in western state of Michoacán attracted a small but dedicated following in rural areas that created a political platform for the transformational presidency of Lázaro Cárdenas, who served as the state's governor from 1928 to 1932. Haciendas that choked off water and cut forests, or intimidated villagers who wanted land, hastened along the process through which certain groups of rural people Michoacán drew upon postrevolutionary ideology and "built for themselves" not a new sense of community, but rather a more materialist sense of oppression and revolutionary redemption associated with their emerging social position as *campesinos*.

Revolution and Nature

Like all social revolutions, Mexico's had complicated origins. The thirty-four-year dictatorship of modernizing strongman (*caudillo*) Porfirio Díaz stabilized the nation's political system for the first time since independence and established the conditions for an unprecedented period of economic expansion based above all on foreign investment in railroads and mining. Yet political stability and economic growth created tensions of their own. The miners and cowboys who migrated from the densely settled villages of central Mexico to the country's rapidly modernizing northern areas left behind the village priests and tight-knit families of their youth. They formed a young, rootless, and potentially restive group that eventually flocked to revolutionary armies during the 1910–1917 conflict. Meanwhile, in the cities and mid-size towns of central Mexico, antiunion legislation and overcrowding made urban life precarious for the emerging sector of industrial workers, whose numbers trended slowly upward and also proved susceptible to the revolution's siren song, albeit not on the scale of their northern counterparts. The middle classes also expanded as the modernization created a demand for accountants, clerks, schoolteachers, and other literate professionals. Yet white-collar workers had few avenues for accumulating wealth. Even some sectors the nation's economic elite found it difficult to break into political life, dominated as it was by Díaz and his coterie of aging cronies.

No group lost more ground during the Díaz years than rural villagers, the impoverished agriculturists who depended on family labor to work modest plots of staple crops, often complemented with casual work elsewhere, who lived in communities known as *pueblos*. An 1856 law that required corporate bodies—villages and ecclesiastical institutions that owned mortmain property to which they had received permanent and inalienable rights of ownership—to privatize their assets and make them available to the open market. The measure initially aimed to force the Church to sell its property in an ostensibly bid to generate more economic activity, though anticlerical politicians also saw this as a means of punishing the Church for its antiliberal politics. The privatization order also pertained to indigenous commons, although it was not widely enforced until the mid-1880s, when the Díaz administration ordered the division of communal property granted to the *pueblos* in the colonial period and the assignment of it to individual villagers. Most communities reluctantly complied, although doing so often led to the loss of land. Some villagers sold their new property to outsiders or wealthy neighbors, while others lost it through tax sales. Sometimes, speculators simply swindled peasants out of their titles. Around the same time, an 1883 law granted survey companies a third of any public land they mapped—a measure intended to make the extent of federal property legible to administrators (who would then be able to make it available in the form of concessions), while placing still more land in circulation. The surveyors did not always take pains to determine who actually owned the land they plotted, and often included indigenous territory within their boundaries. These two modernizing policies resulted in the massive transfer of land from the *pueblos* to hacienda owners and an emerging class of private landowners known as *rancheros*.

The modernizing development of the Díaz years not only divested villagers of their cornfields, it often stripped them of access to natural resources formerly understood as common property. Rural people in the most economically dynamic parts of the country also contended with the commodification of natural resources. The booming economy created markets for goods previously considered valueless or as collective property, such as certain forestlands and waters, and even the debris left over from logging operations in the mountains. For example, landowners in northern Mexico had customarily allowed villagers to glean the "slash" (broken branches, pieces of bark, and unused wood) that loggers left behind after making a cut. Wood gatherers filtered into the mountainside and hauled away the debris, which they fired into charcoal for domestic use and sale in nearby cities. Landowners, meanwhile, benefitted from having potential fuel for forest fires removed from their property. As mining expanded in Sonora, Chihuahua, and Arizona, the regional market for charcoal firmed up, prompting landowners to begin charging for access to their land or, in some instances, to arrange for their own crews to collect the slash. To the wood gatherers, the changes wrought by commodification and the enforcement of property rights verged on the incomprehensible. One Chihuahua muleteer charged with trespassing and wood theft told a judge in 1887 that he could not be convicted because "everyone knows that anyone can use the wood up there."[11]

The use of water also became increasingly contentious in the late nineteenth century and aggravated resource conflicts that in some instances dated back to the colonial era.[12] As the most commercialized haciendas began to function as proto-agribusinesses in central Mexico, their owners invested in irrigation projects that changed regional hydrological regimes. For instance, the Nueva Italia hacienda in Michoacán expanded its holdings by draining a swamp that three peasant villages had used as a source of fish and reeds used to weave sleeping mats. In the state of Morelos, the booming sugar economy induced landowners to irrigate their lands but not to invest in water-saving technologies. Despite one hacienda administrator's lonely call to conserve water, sugar planters drew water from the state's rivers at an unsustainable rate that left some peasant communities scrambling to meet their own needs. Federal officials approved so many permissions to draw water from the Higuerón River, for example, that the sum of water rights exceeded the river's total capacity! Fortunately, most landowners did not exercise their rights and the water continued to flow.[13]

The revolution did not originate as a peasant uprising in response to dispossession, the commodification of resources, or even to a changing moral economy. Instead, the regime unraveled after a political crisis that began when Francisco I. Madero, the scion of a wealthy landowning family sidelined by the regime's hermetic power structures and patrimonial leadership style, ran against the aging dictator in the presidential elections of 1910. Díaz briefly jailed the upstart and declared himself the victor, leading Madero to call for an insurrection. A ragtag uprising of miners, cowboys, and family farmers eventually formed in the nation's north and dealt the federal army a blow that revealed it as a paper tiger. Díaz resigned the following year, but a counter-revolutionary putsch in 1913 led to another two years of fighting that eventually devolved into a civil war between revolutionary factions. Reformist modernizers finally took power and passed a new constitution in 1917. The rural poor joined revolutionary movements in the Atlantic state of Veracruz, the northern state Durango, and elsewhere, particularly before revolutionary armies became professionalized in 1914/1915. The most significant peasant movement came together under the leadership of Emiliano Zapata in the central-south state of Morelos, where the expansion of sugar plantations squeezed land away from many *pueblos*, even as proletarianized peasants working in the sugar fields grew increasingly restive.[14]

Zapata was among the first to respond to Madero's appeal for a revolutionary uprising in 1910. Until his death in 1919, he led peasants from Morelos and the adjacent state of Puebla in a bid to recover resources that the *pueblos* had lost to sugar planters. Historians have tended to overestimate Zapatismo's military significance—although the Morelos peasant fighters did occupy the nation's capital for most of 1915—and to romanticize its accomplishments. But while Zapata's movement may not have changed the course of armed conflict, it left an indelible symbolic mark on how political leaders and *campesinos* remembered the revolution and sought to realize its legacy. Zapata's signature political manifesto—the Plan of Ayala—became an unofficial declaration of revolutionary principles in the countryside. It held that "*pueblos* or citizens" that had unimpeachable titles to "the fields, timber, and water which the landlords, *científicos,* or bosses have usurped" could immediately recover them and defend them with armed force if necessary. Moreover, one-third of the land, timber, and water held by "monopolists" would be expropriated and delivered to peasants who lacked such titles.[15] This document, written with the collaboration of a local schoolteacher, became both guiding principle of Zapata's movement and an inspiration to the rural poor in other revolutionary movements who hoped that the revolution would somehow grant them access not only to land but to other natural resources as well.

These expectations took a huge step toward realization when a radical faction of delegates took control of the constitutional convention convened in 1916 and succeeded in ramming through progressive articles that guaranteed the right to land reform, labor unions, and universal education and healthcare. For the next two decades, Mexican political leaders took halting steps to realize these "revolutionary promises" as reformist governments sought desperately to manage a nation divided between a generally conservative populace punctuated by pockets of radical workers, peasants, and politicians. Land reform got off to a slow start, with many peasants hesitating to request land because they doubted whether the policies would endure for long, because they knew that the Church opposed it and that most landowners would not part with their property without a fight. But the genie had escaped the bottle. For the next two decades, small cadres peasants pressed their demands not only for cornfields, but for water and forests as well. Landowners and most clergymen dug in and mounted a vigorous opposition, supported by much of the political establishment and a sizeable proportion of the rural population. Nevertheless, agrarians frequently received support from radical politicians, many of whom regarded land reform as the central front of a broader class struggle against the forces of "counterrevolution." For them, land and nature itself constituted a key weapon in what was at root a rural class struggle that pitted poor peasants against wealthy landowners.

Postrevolutionary Radicalism and the Invention of the *Campesino* "Class"

Mexico in the wake of the revolution became a global beacon for radical politics. Mexico City in particular became a hothouse of left-wing politics. Artists like Tina Modotti, Edward Weston, and Sergei Eisenstein visited and mingled with the great Mexican painters such as Diego Rivera, Frida Kahlo, and José Clemente Orozco. Labor "internationalists" visited from the United States, Spain, and Italy to give speeches in favoring unions and labor militancy, and occasionally sought to mobilize workers and in some cases field hands. The nation's presidents generally slid rightward during the 1920s, as their support for land reform and (autonomous) organized labor waned.[16] Yet grassroots militancy appeared in several pockets of the countryside, particularly where the villagers who solicited land reform parcels suffered reprisals from landowners. In some states, radical governors—many of whom defined themselves as socialists—approved of agrarian radicalism for ideological reasons and because well disciplined peasant supporters made formidable political clients. Governors such as Adalberto Tejada of Veracruz, Salvador Alvarado of Yucatán, Tomás Garrido Canibal of Tabasco, and others attempted—with varying degrees of success—to leverage peasant support into political capital.

Two governors of the state of Michoacán also became significant voices on the revolutionary left. Fransciso J. Múgica (1920–1922) and Lázaro Cárdenas (1928–1932) governed the state at the unsettled moment during which an increasingly radicalized agrarian movement pressed for land reform in the face of determined resistance from landowners and, between 1926 and 1929, counterrevolutionary Catholic peasant rebels known as *cristeros*. Both governors depicted peasants as members of the proletariat and saw the land reform as a process of turning the means of production over to the so-called rural workers. Socialist-inspired prose suffused their official discourse. Múgica's official mouthpiece declared in 1920, for example, that "the eternally exploited workers have always been the first to join the battle to vindicate human rights [*los derechos del hombre*]; these workers of the fields and shop floors have bathed the battlefields with their blood."[17]

A few years later Cárdenas's secretary of education referred to the popular classes—in a typical refrain for the era—as "workers, laborers, and *campesinos*" rather than the more common prerevolutionary terms such as rural poor, or Indians, or "villagers [*el pueblo*]."[18] The governor's workers' union-cum-political machine (aptly named the Michoacán Revolutionary Confederation of Labor) stated as its first principle that it "Recognized that Land and its fruits belong to those who work it directly; therefore, one of this organization's primary goals is to realize a broad solution to the agrarian Problem by giving *campesinos* the land to which they have a right."[19]

Rural people recognized in this purple revolutionary prose a potentially valuable tool to cement their claims on the land. Some no doubt deployed the language of revolutionary justice strategically, as a means of ingratiating themselves to political leaders. Others appear to have taken it to heart. Correspondence from rural Mexicans of this era is notoriously difficult to interpret because so few villagers could write and depended instead on literate figures in the countryside, including schoolteachers, priests, and the itinerant scribes known as *tintorillos*, but the sheer number of documents in which rural people made reference to images of class struggle suggests that the language of labor and social justice pervaded the countryside. In many cases, the language of class comingled with older ideas of religiosity and divine justice. For example, a barely legible letter that villagers sent to Michoacán's agrarian league from 1924 concluded, "Lord God, judge of the quick and the dead, sole master of all living creatures, made the earth for everyone and excluding no one. Therefore, [hacienda owners should not] keep the great supreme government from redistributing land to the nation, to each individual, so that we can be the masters of our own labor."[20] One group of agrarians and hacienda field whom Cárdenas visited in 1934 complained of landowner malfeasance and defined themselves to him as "organized workers, widows, and orphans," for example.[21] A political militant and ardent supporter of Cárdenas in the conservative Zamora district drove the point home by referring to himself and his followers as "authentic workers" and his political enemies as false leaders and "Judases who for a long time now have sold out our brothers for thirty coins of TREACHERY."[22]

The imbrication of profane and divine understandings of justice suggests that they existed on the same conceptual plane in at least some people's minds. Religion had helped to bind villagers together for centuries, of course. Now the bonds of community were defined in class terms as well, in a Thompsonian transfer of one solidarity to another.

Rural radicalism did not exist solely on the plane of language and representation, of course. The ideas of social justice, antihacienda militancy, and even anticlericalism often translated into practice as well. The parish priest from the *pueblo* of Taretan, whose mixed-race (mestizo) population worked as field hands in the adjacent hacienda, described the community as "a peaceful refuge" until some of the young men received a scholarship to attend the La Huerta normal school outside Morelia, an institution known for its radical pedagogy overseen by the famous communist headmistress, María del Refugio (Cuca) García. "What an education!" lamented the priest, "impious, atheist, and wicked [*malvada*] in every respect." Indeed, the priest concluded that he was witnessing an irreversible shift in local political culture. He concluded that, "These young men from the famous La Huerta school have taken over the government of this *pueblo* through the most crass means and to the indignation of honorable residents.... Since they came to power through imposition rather than election, everyone here opposes them, the hacienda owners have expressed their indignation at these outrages by halting production on their property, leaving the villagers in abject poverty.... Since the people here are ignorant and simple workers, it is easy [for the radicals] to snatch them away and gain new followers ... who are beginning to lose respect for the clergy."[23] These narratives of loss and regret appeared repeatedly in Catholic thought of the postrevolutionary era,[24] but they also attest to the occasional success of local agrarian leaders in building a base of support, particularly when landowners turned against their workers and intimidated them with force or, in this case, economic suasion.

The Ecology of Postrevolutionary Class Conflict

The use of nature as a weapon to prosecute the agrarian conflict became increasingly common during the postrevolutionary era. Hacienda owners "accidentally" allowed too little (or too much) water into irrigation ditches on what had once been their land. Unexplained fires raced over terrain scheduled for redistribution to peasant communities. Forests disappeared in contested areas despite prohibitions on logging any land whose ownership was under adjudication. Although these were far from the only sources of conflict between landowners and *campesinos* during the early phases of land reform, many villagers found them particularly nettlesome. *Campesinos* who had requested land reform parcels chafed not only at the loss of their soon-to-be resources, but also at the idea that hacienda owners would rather destroy the land than hand it over. Weaponizing nature for use in a "class" conflict suggested that the postrevolutionary discourses that painted landowners as implacable enemies of *campesinos* had a basis in practice. Moreover, it helped to open the way for a new form of postrevolutionary logic that suggested that *campesinos* had a right to the land not only because they tilled it and had experienced a collective heritage of dispossession, but because they were better stewards of nature itself.

Agrarian reform involved not only the land itself, but also the resources that made it flourish. It is not surprising that these resources became the source of conflict in their own right. In 1925, for example, a conflict erupted between the village of Turicato and the San Rafael hacienda. The two entities had shared water from the same irrigation canal, which drew from the Río

Caliente and crossed the hacienda before delivering the water that villagers used for washing, cooking, and watering their orchards. Although no one agreed who had originally built the canal—one suspects the hacienda had organized construction and the locals provided labor—it had become customary for villagers to dredge the whole length of the waterway, from the intake flume at the river all the way to the village. The landowners, however, began to suspect that villagers had designs on their lands and refused entry to them. In October 1925, tree branches and other debris clogged the canal, and Turicato's water dried up. When villagers crossed onto the hacienda to clear the obstruction, however, the administrator chased them off.[25]

Turicato was located in one of the most socially and politically conservative districts of the state. The predominantly mestizo population included a substantial population of small, independent farmers known as *rancheros* who almost universally opposed land reform and anticlericalism. The agrarian movement was associated with a small group of firebrands who had formed a militia in town (most likely inspired by the village schoolteacher) to support Governor Múgica's proagrarian administration and to combat what its leaders described as religious "fanaticism" in the area, by which they apparently meant the village priest's habit of sermonizing that the agrarian reform represented nothing less than a sin: the theft of private property. After the conflict over water, more villagers began to question the status quo and consider supporting the small local cadre of agrarian activists.[26] Indeed, conflicts over water—and landowners' assertions to be the sole arbiters of how and where it should be used—helped drive agrarian radicalism in several parts of the state.[27]

Sometimes, the fight over water involved not the immediate threat of deprivation, but rather threats to the hydrological regime as a result of misuse. Most Mexicans believed that deforestation reduced the overall level of rainfall and made natural springs dry up. As rural people became increasingly aware of this so-called desiccation theory during the 1930s, they began to worry that landowners who overcut their woods were also responsible for all manner of ecological damage. One set of villagers complained, for example, that a hacienda owner who cut trees in the Senguío River watershed was responsible for diminished rainfalls and halving its overall flow.[28]

More commonly, villagers complained that landowners (or "counterrevolutionary" neighboring communities) were responsible for intentionally cutting trees on territories slated for redistribution through the land reform process. In at least some instances, such fears were well founded. Property owners learned which lands villagers had requested with a reasonable degree of certainty because surveyors often contacted them before mapping out land reform parcels. The law prohibited landowners from using the woods after that point, but in practice there were few if any sanctions to stop them. Because the forest service had little traction in most parts of the countryside, it fell to land reform beneficiaries to police their own soon-to-be property and file complaints if hacienda owners tried to harvest timber beforehand. When landowners succeeded in harvesting the timber, villagers received not the valuable woodlots they hoped would sustain them for years to come, or perhaps even indefinitely, but rather erosion-prone pasturelands that held virtually no value.

Conclusion

The advent of land reform in the wake of the Mexican Revolution, particularly in states like Michoacán that had not been a central stage of revolutionary upheaval, had complex effects on rural society. It rewrote the moral economy by breaking down the mutual dependency between haciendas and villages that had survived through the nineteenth century, in which villagers complemented their subsistence agriculture by taking occasional casual work on haciendas, which for their own part encroached upon but did not typically destroy the *pueblos*.[29] Moreover, it undermined cultural understandings about land ownership, vitiating older liberal ideals (buttressed in important ways by the Catholic Church) that naturalized the rights to private property and hence of landowners' access to natural resources. Land reform reframed the issue of property holding and defined it not as an inalienable (and religiously sanctioned) right based on the principle of private property, but rather as an issue of social justice. This reconfiguration of *rights* and *justice* placed the rural poor in a new category of people known as *campesinos* who had their own moral claims upon natural resources by virtue of their relative poverty.

The cases in which landowners responded to land reform by squandering natural resources or overtly sabotaging the land represented something more than the theft of goods from rural communities that hoped to receive valuable property. Rather, it constituted a weaponization of nature for use in the ongoing "class" struggle against *campesinos* and the governments that supported them. Contests over the forests and streams opened a significant new front in the already conflictive relationship between people who increasingly identified themselves as *campesinos*—poor rural people who had both moral and constitutional rights to the land—and landowners excoriated in postrevolutionary ideology as enemies of the revolution and of "rural workers" generally.

One intriguing consequence of landowners' willingness to destroy or compromise waterways and forests was that it established the conceptual basis for a rhetoric that defined *campesinos*, rather than large landowners, as the social sector with the greatest sense of responsibility to conserve natural resources. Peasants already had a storehouse of local knowledge about how to use nature, of course, and they retained many of their ancestral practices even after the revolution. They were not "nature conservationists," and in many cases were themselves responsible for deforestation, poor soil management practices, and other practices that degraded the environment.

Nevertheless, Lázaro Cárdenas, the former governor of Michoacán who became president in 1934, took steps to inculcate scientific ideas of sustained-yield forestry and soil conservation in the countryside. In many ways, his policies anticipated the ideals of community-based stewardship of the land promoted by the ecology movement of the 1970s. The idea that hacienda owners had become the enemies, not only of *campesinos*, but of nature itself, helped set the stage for rural people's acceptance of the Cardenista gospel of conservation and rational use of resources. In the shorter term, it suggests that new Thompsonian bonds of cohesion within land reform communities were built not only on issues of class antagonism that divided the rural poor and hacienda owners, but on an emerging ideal that *campesinos* were the best possible protectors of Mexican nature and hence deserved to become its stewards.

***Christopher Boyer** is Dean of Arts and Letters and Professor of History at Northern Arizona University. He specializes in the social and environmental history of Modern Mexico and Latin America. His most recent book,* Political Landscapes: Forests, Conservation, and Community in Mexico *(Duke University Press) investigates the social history of Mexican forest management between 1880 and 2000. His current book project traces how Green Revolution technologies pioneered in Mexico in the 1950s served to promote the industrialization of foodways in Mexico and the developing world. He co-edits a University of Arizona Press book series on Latin American environmental history.*

Notes

1. E. P. Thompson, *The Making of the English Working Class* (New York: Vintage Books, 1966), 405.
2. Ibid., 447.
3. Christopher R. Boyer, "The Threads of Class at La Virgen: Misrepresentation and Identity at a Mexican Textile Mill, 1918–1935," *American Historical Review* 105, no. 5 (2000): 1576–1598.
4. The historiography on these topics is vast. Important introductions include François-Xavier Guerra, *México: Del antiguo régimen a la Revolución*, 2 vols. (Mexico City: Fondo de Cultura Económica, 1988); Gilbert M. Joseph, *Revolution from Without: Yucatán, Mexico, and the United States, 1880–1924* (Durham, NC: Duke University Press, 1988); and John Lear, *Workers, Neighbors, and Citizens: The Revolution in Mexico City* (Lincoln: University of Nebraska Press, 2001).
5. Christopher R. Boyer, *Becoming Campesinos: Politics, Identity, and Agrarian Struggle in Postrevolutionary Michoacán, 1920–1935* (Stanford, CA: Stanford University Press, 2003), 20–25, 212–217.
6. Classic studies of agrarian contention include Paul Friedrich, *Agrarian Revolt in a Mexican Village*, with a new preface (Chicago: University of Chicago Press, 1977); Jesús Silva Herzog, *El agrarismo mexicano y la reforma agraria. Exposición y crítica* (Mexico City: Fondo de Cultura Económica, 1959).

7. Few historians of Mexico have attempted to understand how the landscape becomes embedded into class struggle. For a notable exception, see Myrna I. Santiago, *The Ecology of Oil: Environment, Labor, and the Mexican Revolution, 1900–1938* (Cambridge: Cambridge University Press, 2006).
8. In addition to Boyer's *Becoming Campesinos*, see Paul K. Eiss, *In the Name of El Pueblo: Place, Community, and the Politics of History in Yucatán* (Durham, NC: Duke University Press, 2010); Guillermo Palacios, *La pluma y el arado. Los intelectuales pedagogos y la construcción sociocultural del "problema campesino" en México, 1932–1934* (Mexico City: El Colegio de México/CIDE, 1999).
9. E. P. Thompson, "The Moral Economy of the English Crowd in the Eighteenth Century," *Past & Present* 50, no. 1 (1971): 76–136; Eric R. Wolf, "Aspects of Group Relations in a Complex Society: Mexico," *American Anthropologist*, New Series, 8, no. 6 (1956): 1065–1078.
10. Thompson, *The Making*, 10.
11. Testimony of Juan Gutiérrez, 5 October [should be September] 1887, Centro de Investigaciones de Chihuahua, Biblioteca Pública Central Estatal (Chihuahua City), Ramo Batopilas, Fondo Porfiriato y Terracismo, Sección Justicia, caja 3, exp. 39.
12. Sonia Lipsett-Rivera, *To Defend Our Water with the Blood of Our Veins: The Struggle for Resources in Colonial Puebla* (Albuquerque: University of New Mexico Press, 1999).
13. Alejandro Tortolero Villaseñor, "Water and Revolution in Morelos, 1850–1915," in *A Land between Waters: Environmental Histories of Modern Mexico*, ed. Christopher R. Boyer (Tucson: University of Arizona Press, 2012), 124–149.
14. Paul Hart, *Bitter Harvest: The Social Transformation of Morelos, Mexico, and the Origins of the Zapatista Revolution, 1840–1910* (Albuquerque: University of New Mexico Press, 2007); John Womack, Jr., *Zapata and the Mexican Revolution* (New York: Knopf, 1968).
15. As quoted in Womack, *Zapata*, 400.
16. Jürgen Buchenau, *Plutarco Elías Calles and the Mexican Revolution* (Lanham, MD: Rowman and Littlefield, 2007), 143–172.
17. *El Heraldo de Michoacán* (Morelia), 10 June 1920.
18. Circular bulletin from Celso Flores Zamora, 15 January 1930, Archivo Municipal de Zamora, Sección Instrucción Pública, 1930, exp. 10.
19. "Estatutos Confederales: CRMDT 1931," Morelia, June 1931, 2.
20. The verbatim quote (errors and all) reads: "El Sr. Dios Juez de Bibos y Muertos Dueño Unico, detodo, lo criado, y hizo la Tierra, Paratodos y Anadie labendio; Por que Adetener Elgran supremo, gobierno, Enrepartirle, Ala Nacian y Acadauno, supedaso detierra Para que todos cean Dueños de sutrabajo, y Fabor de Resolvernos lomas pronto, Pocible, Para saber losfines." Paz Rodríguez to Gildardo Magaña, 11 October 1924, Archivo General de la Nación (hereafter AGN), Ramo Departamento del Trabajo, caja 726, exp. 4.
21. "Trabajadores" to Cárdenas, 19 July 1934 AGN, Ramo Dirección General del Gobierno (hereafter DGG), 2.331.8 (13)–8, caja 29A, exp. 9.
22. Federación Distrital Agraria y Sindicalista de Zamora to President of the Republic, 23 April 1933, AGN-DGG, 2.331.9 (13)–4, caja 61A, exp. 3.
23. Report of Pbro. Telésforo Gómez, 12–17 May 1931, Archivo de la Catedal de Zamora, exp. "Taretan VII-1929-V-1936."
24. For more, see Ben Fallaw, *Religion and State Formation in Postrevolutionary Mexico* (Durham, NC: Duke University Press, 2013); Manuel Ceballos Ramírez, *El*

Catolicismo Social: Un tercero en discordia. Rerum Novarum, *la "cuestión social" y la movilización de los católicos mexicanos (1891–1911)* (Mexico City: El Colegio de México, 1991).

25. Archivo Histórico del Poder Eejecutivo de Michoacán, ramo Amparos, caja 236, exp. 2.
26. For example, miembros de la defensa to Múgica, 22 January 1922, AGN-DGG, C.2.51–17 (caja 21).
27. Boyer, *Campesinos,* 96–98; Friedrich, *Agrarian Revolt,* 45–48.
28. AGN-ramo Secretaría de Agricultura y Recursos Hidraúlicos, caja 1–1, exp. 107 leg. 2.
29. Alan Knight, *The Mexican Revolution,* vol. 1. *Porfirians, Liberals, and Peasants* (Lincoln: University of Nebraska Press, 1990), 82–91.

Chapter 4

Worst Conceivable Form

Race, Global Capital, and The Making of the English Working Class

Zach Sell

Following the intellectual revolution of Karl Marx, a series of black radical and anticolonial critiques have argued that the destructive violence of capital has been seriously underestimated. Neither Marx nor Engels, writing at the heart of empire, were prepared to predict or fully understand the racial techniques of capital in the colonial period. As Frantz Fanon insisted in *The Wretched of the Earth,* the fact of colonialism demanded that everything be thought again.[1] From one perspective, E. P. Thompson's *The Making of the English Working Class* appears to exist in nonrelation to such demands for rethinking capitalism: he envisions it being made at a remove from both the transnational circuits of capital and the colonial projects themselves. For Thompson, the intimate experience of togetherness during the Industrial Revolution gives the English working class its history. Its relationship to "the greater part of the world" emerges only in terms of analogy. The English history of Industrial Revolution is a kind of first history that has global utility by providing an ideal type for the greater part of the world "still undergoing problems of industrialization."[2]

Fifty years after *The Making*'s publication, we still know little about the correspondences between the English working class and the transnational spaces of capital and colonialism.[3] As Thompson noted, the first half of the nineteenth century was a period of immense pain; along these transnational circuits this pain was lived differently. In England, political discourse, ranging from radical to conservative, according to Thompson, offered "the sense of some catastrophic change,"[4] but the contours of this catastrophe went far beyond England—an issue not addressed by Thompson. In the first half of the nineteenth century, capitalism expressed itself through racial exploitation and the imposition of colonialism with particular viciousness: The United States grew as whites ethnically cleansed the American South, clearing ground for plantation slavery just as the factory system grew. The explosive nexus between Lancashire and the American South, combined with British colonial policies in India, dismantled Bengal's handloom textile industry.[5] By 1828, Bengal had lost its position to export to England.[6] This dismantling coincided with the East India Company increasingly looking to India as a site for the further development of plantation agriculture and the colonial extraction of resources.

In consideration of this explosive nexus, this article draws on W. E. B. Du Bois's writing on correspondence within capitalism in order to expand upon Thompson's notion of working-class consciousness. In his important history of the black diaspora, *The Negro*, Du Bois noted that the cotton-producing slave plantation in the United States "corresponds" to the modern factory in its "worst conceivable form."[7] Interposed between owners and enslaved laborers were overseers and drivers who whipped and drove slaves within a pseudo-mechanized task system. The territorial extension of this system south and west was part of the "world-conquering vision" of slave masters. Du Bois's use of the term corresponds, rather than other terms such as "is analogous to" is deliberate: it entails communicative exchange which analogy lacks. Correspondence also suggests coordinated relation that undercuts the formal comparative equivalence of analogy.[8] Beyond this, correspondence enables consideration of relation beyond spatial proximity and does not foreclose existing social relation even as the process of correspondence produces relational change.

This article reinserts correspondence and its cognates into the grammar of the anticolonial and antiracist critique of capital. Southern settler slavery, Lancashire textile factories, and colonial India "corresponded" through the fantasies of capital and the English working class. Organizing the article to respond to Thompson's claim that the working class "ma[de] itself as much as it was made," the section "World-Conquering Visions" presents the political and economic fantasies of the architects of factory production, colonial domination, and settler slavery as the formative antithesis of working class self-making.[9] To do so, the article expands upon Marx's insight that capital is not inanimate and necessarily implies the capitalist. For Marx, the capitalist was not simply the factory owner but also included the Southern planter because of his position within the capitalist world market as structured through English factory labor.[10] From this perspective, I also consider the writings of governor general of India William Bentinck, who looked at settler colonialism in the United States and factory production in metropolitan England as he pursued colonial improvement in India. The second section, "Radical Consciousness, Racial Consciousness," examines the ways in which the English republican radical Richard Carlile's views on race and economy corresponded with slavery in the United States and Jamaica as well as with Orientalist considerations of Islam and Hinduism. Together, these two sections insert the implications of race and colonialism into the culture of global capital in the first half of the nineteenth century.

World-Conquering Visions

Correspondences emerge in the ideas of a racial political economy applied by nineteenth-century theorists of factory, plantation, and colonial expansion. In his writing on cotton manufacture, Andrew Ure looked toward handloom production in colonial Bengal to articulate the significance of the factory through the language of imperial manhood. In his argument for the expansion of a white permanent settlement in India's colonial interior, Governor General Bentinck refined his vision by making a correspondence with the white settler revolt in colonial America. Organizations like the Agricultural and Horticultural Society of India (AHSI) saw the connection between the American South and British India and entered into a process of correspondence and exchange that sought to move techniques from the Southern plantation to colonial India. Eminent slave owners such as James Henry Hammond observed this process and developed their arguments about the particularity of American white supremacy and settler slavery within capitalism. Each assessment might be rendered as part of a particular racial or colonial project, yet all were held together not only by circuits of capital but also by transnational racial practices and assessments. Drawing insights from classical political economy, these theorists formulated visions that race, climate, and colonial encounters could suspend the rules of capital as commonly theorized.[11]

Andrew Ure studied anatomy at Edinburgh and Glasgow before relocating to London, where he made significant contributions to debates over factory organization and management. In Marx's *Capital*, Ure is the bourgeois "Philosopher of Factory" against whom some of Marx's most powerful ideas unfold. His *Philosophy of Manufacture* is among the most significant works within the discourse about the factory system in the early nineteenth century and has caused him to be seen as a precursor of Fredrick Winslow Taylor's scientific management. The factory system, as Thompson noted, was a "crime" that thrived through the beating, torture, and exploitation of children in textile mills. Ure was at the forefront of those who were apologists for these crimes in the nineteenth century.[12]

In his lesser-known two-volume *The Cotton Manufactures of Great Britain,* Ure surveyed cotton textile production methods and was especially attentive to Indian handloom production. For Ure, the transformation of textile manufacture in England was an assertion of imperial white manhood. Textile production was under "long but graceful pupilage in the plains of Hindustan, till its recent growth into a gigantic manhood under the fostering genius of Great Britain."[13] The pairing of gigantic manhood with genius posited nationhood, through manual and intellectual labor, against a virility that pastoral Indian handloom production could not match. English virility gave meaning to the factory in terms of culture and class in ways that could not be unlinked. Factory production was empowered by and empowering to English masculinity; it made the island gigantic compared to its colonial possession despite geographic differences in size.

Ure's account also mitigated the complexities of caste, region, religion, and trade within handloom production and reduced this complexity to "Mahometans" and "Hindoo women." The latter were especially important in the calculation of difference between factory and colonial textile production.[14] The most delicate textiles were spun by Hindoo women, who had a "temperament" that would be "[d]escribed under the title of *nervous* by modern physiologists."[15] The "Hindoo constitution" was characterized by an "excess of sensibility in the ordinary transactions of life." This excess of sensibility was visible in the body: "pliant limbs and fingers, a pathetic look; a feeling of anxiety attendant upon the play of organs; lively sensations occasioned by very slight causes."[16] The reduction of complex social differences to Hindoo women established a set of coordinates for describing the triumph of the factory in terms of gendered civilizational conquest—white men conquered the nervous constitution of Hindoo women. The nervousness of Hindu women spinners was part of larger colonial discourses on South Asia focused upon bodily degeneration, which, as Tanika Sarkar has noted, centered on the bodily degeneration of the Hindu male babu.[17]

According to one scholar of Ure, *The Philosophy of Manufacture* aspired to describe a capitalist Utopia characterized by an automatic factory without workers.[18] In contrast, *The Cotton Manufactures* attempted to ameliorate metropolitan class antagonisms. Nothing was more important to the rise of Great Britain's textile industry than its "race of laborious, skilful, and inventive artisans, cherished as they have been by the institutions of a free country, which opened to the possessors of talents and knowledge, in however humble a station, the amplest career of honour and fortune to stimulate effort and dignify success."[19] Free English artisans who entered the factory built a triumphant industry that unmanly colonial production could not match. Ure also compared the labor of free men to colonial slavery in the Caribbean, noting, "The reluctant tasks of our colonial slaves have been converted into the cheerful labours of freemen."[20] Materially and ideologically the factory represented the triumph of freedom and the extension of colonial power.

The comparative impulse provided Ure with a way to understand factory and manhood through British Empire. Bentinck, whose imperial practice was guided by the practical application of utilitarian principles to colonial rule, was informed by a political economy based upon racial assessments of "the Native" within settler dynamics in North America and colonial India. In his 30 May 1829 Minute, Bentinck argued for the expansion of permanent white settlement into the Indian interior. This argument was based upon a belief in the racial benefit of expanded settlement to the economy. This benefit was contrasted to the settler colonial revolt in North America, which disrupted the free flow of wealth from colony and empire.[21] The Minute presented colonial superiority as undeniable: the presence of white English men would result in the "diffusion" of European skill and the development of colonial India. National character and national wealth were directly related through the uplifting presence of expanded white settlement.[22]

The strongest argument for expanded permanent settlement could be found in the "annihilation" of the cotton market by English manufacture. Expanded white settlement was necessary because of the particularly devastating impact that "European skill and machinery" produced against the "prosperity of India."[23] The only substantive developments in manufacture and agriculture that had occurred recently were English, as the growing of improved species of tobacco and the establishment of a steam-powered cotton-twist factory demonstrated. Beyond this, there was a state of general degradation except for indigo planters, who—though criticized for excess—had improved the colonial economy and Native character by establishing plantations for the export of raw materials.[24]

That the transition of Anglo settlers in the United States from colonial to independent sovereign subjects affected how white settlement expanded in colonial India was well understood. Bentinck addressed the fear that colonial India would follow the fate of colonial America: "the original inhabitants of the country would be subjected to violence and oppression; and ... the colonists, if not swept away by insurrections of their own creating would soon claim independence, and assume an attitude of hostility to England."[25] If British subjects could settle freely in India, their presence would replicate the United States—a dramatic failure in negotiating the interests between Native and settler subjects.[26]

Bentinck argued that there was "no analogy" between "the Natives" and settlers in North America and colonial India. To do so, he established differences in climate, property, and economy, each with an attendant racial logic.[27] As part of the tropics, India would not become a place for the permanent settlement of white laborers from England because their racial constitution would cause them to "perish."[28] A large surplus population of Native labor made white labor unnecessary. Settlers would be comprised of men of "capital and skill" rather than all classes, as had been the case in the American colonies. The property rights of colonial subjects in India would not be abrogated because property was fully delineated, unlike in North America. This ahistorical distinction recalled the theoretical stance within British colonialism visible in the liberalism of Locke ("the uncultivated wast[e] of America"), which rendered Native North America "wild" and available for cultivating settlement.[29] The logic that undergirded Bentinck's perspective suggested that expanded white settlement in colonial America disrupted mechanisms of imperial capital accumulation that were dependent on surplus population for the extraction of value.[30] It is significant to note that the fundamental problem for Bentinck was not genocide, but that genocide, insurrection, and revolt could make surplus population unavailable. Bentinck's work to articulate a different colonialism reflected a white supremacist political economic imaginary that assessed differential values for Native labor within American settler and South Asian colonial contexts to refine imperial capitalism.[31]

Marking Hinduism and Islam as distinct religious communities provided Bentinck with evidence of changeable Native racial characteristics. *Zamindars* who identified as Muslim despite "trac[ing] origins to a Hindoo ancestor" presented ample evidence of this changeable character.[32] Further, industrious Natives were "accustomed to all kinds of severe toil" and would provide colonial manufacturers and planters with "a singularly cheap supply of labour."[33] Rather than rebelling, Native subjects would "accomodat[e] themselves to the various tempers of their masters."[34] By inference, this differed from North America, where the conquest and theft of land rendered Native life as superfluous rather than as a surplus population necessary for labor.

Bentinck's vision of expanded permanent settlement was based on differentiating settler colonialism in North America from expanded white settlement in colonial India. He relied upon a racialized political economic vision that was capable of differentiating the relation between Native, settler, colony, empire, and capital in the past from a future that would cause these interests to more perfectly align. To do so, he deployed a vision of racial political economy informed by climate and difference that, in the case of India, would make for a successful colonial policy for the extraction of raw materials. To establish the differing racial tractability of Native populations in North America and colonial India was to assess the possibilities for making subordinate surplus labor.

Shifting India into the tropics within colonial discourse was critical for imagining a hierarchically differentiated capitalist economy between zones of factory and plantation production.[35] As designated zones for the production of raw materials, the American South and colonial India were drawn into correspondence with one another by the AHSI, which transferred Bourbon, Sea Island, and Upland Georgia cotton seed as well as Maryland and Virginia tobacco from the American South to colonial India. These seemingly mundane exchanges were part of the further consolidation of hierarchically and racially differentiated spaces of production, with India reconceived as a place for the production of raw materials suited for metropolitan consumption. This reordering was intimately bound to the dynamic between colony and capital. Based in Calcutta, AHSI worked in tandem with the East India Company, zamindars, and collectors in an attempt to transform India into a site of plantation production. This exchange began first with seed and later developed into the movement of personnel between the American South and British India just as AHSI corresponded with the South Carolina Agricultural Society to gain information about Southern plantation practices.[36]

The efforts by the AHSI and the East India Company to learn from and supplant American cotton plantations were noted by a Southern slave master James Henry Hammond. In 1841, Hammond addressed the South Carolina Agricultural Society, placing the state of South Carolina within the broader Southern plantation economy. The speech was given as the economy reeled from the depressed price of cotton, which had not recovered from the Panic of 1837. In this context, Hammond worked to think through ways the South as a region would emerge from crisis. He also addressed the South's particularity to the global plantation economy in relation to Conquest, the Liverpool cotton market, and to the East India Company's effort to expand cotton production in colonial India.

The Panic of 1837 required a searching assessment and demonstrated the ways in which US settler slavery had become fused to circuits of finance, commercial, and productive capital.[37] Hammond noted that land speculation and credit were the cause of the South's economic depression. Empire gave England "command" of commerce necessary for a "manufacturing revolution," but the South was uniquely positioned to provide raw materials, especially cotton, because of its plantation economy based upon slavery and conquest of productive land.[38]

It was impossible for colonial India to take the United States' place in cotton production given the crucial difference between settler slavery and colonialism in South Asia.[39] "With a soil impoverished by 2000 years or more of cultivation; ... with an idle and feeble race of labourers; paralyzed by absurd social forms; and subjected to the most unprofitable as well as the most wretched system of slavery; with all these drawbacks, I cannot believe that India will be able to compete with us."[40] Hammond was profoundly invested in the unique power of white supremacy through settler slavery in the American South and convinced on the grounds of a revision to classical political economy of this uniqueness. From Hammond's perspective, white settlers in the South had struggled to erase Native presence to provide a clearing for civilizing institutions. Ancient and despotic forms of slavery in colonial India were not created by white men and did not enact the racial uplift that accompanied chattel slavery—an institution providing racial and civilizational uplift for Africans. The American South had "the finest soil" and climate upon which black labor cultivated the earth and black people were cultivated by white mastery.[41] Black labor managed by white men was superior to an "idle and feeble race" in colonial India unmastered and unmanaged by whites.

Even in times of bust, Hammond still believed in the possibility of boom through settlement and enslavement; he looked toward the Republic of Texas in particular. He noted that the "adventurous offspring of the Anglo-Saxon family" had rescued from a "slothful race" the region between the Sabine and Rio Grande rivers.[42] These white men would be capable of supplying cotton to the entire human family through their mastery of enslaved black labor. His calculations of the aftermath of Conquest in Louisiana, Mississippi, Alabama, and Florida noted that with 130 million areas of cultivatable land, coupled with the Republic of Texas, the American South could supply the entire world at present and into the future with cotton. The ability of white settlers in the American South to use the violence of conquest and to repopulate Texas through the internal slave trade provided assurance of the continued centrality that slave owning in the American South would have to the global economy. The South's ability to combine conquest, black slavery, and white mastery was unmatched by any other colonial project and was therefore indispensable to industrial capital.[43]

At the base of Hammond, Bentinck, and Ure's assessments was a series of procedures that broke down laboring and colonized populations racially into hierarchically differentiated categories with different productive potentials. In the process, these categories offered an applied vision of racialized political economy that was influenced by classical political economy even as the tropics of colonial India and "warmer climates" of the American South created exceptions to the general rules that classical political economy established.[44] For all, though differently, the factory marked the triumph of white men's productive power. While there were numerous contradictions in such assessments that often turned upon separate visions of who would be "white masters of the world" (to borrow again from Du Bois), each gestured toward the way in which racial assessment and the economy corresponded.[45] These fantasies of dominance provided theories for the world historical practices of exploitation that subaltern laborers were forced to confront. As Thompson also argued, the working class *was made* as much as it made itself.[46]

Radical Consciousness, Racial Consciousness

The conventional notion of a racially segregated Atlantic world, in which black people were confined to English colonial regions and never appeared in the metropole, has been challenged in recent years. The "rehabilitation" of black radical England as well as work on slavery and antislavery's constitutive impact on working-class consciousness has been formidable. Robert

Wedderburn went from being dismissingly seen as a "coloured tailor" and "last Spencean" to an organic intellectual of anti-slavery and Atlantic revolution.[47] Unnoticed radical networks have been reconstructed and hidden relations revealed. Olaudah Equiano, the once enslaved abolitionist, wrote at least part of his *Interesting Narrative* at the home of Thomas Hardy (the London Corresponding Society founder and first secretary with whom *The Making* begins).[48] These rehabilitations and reconstructions have done much to undercut any vision of a spatially or racially segregated Atlantic.

Like the spaces of capital, "English" working-class consciousness was messy and extended beyond the nation, forming in correspondence with colonial projects. In his description of burgeoning class consciousness, Thompson noted that the 1820s were a period within which radicalism was "an intellectual culture" with dramatic moments of workers' self-education.[49] Significant figures within this intellectual culture included John Wade, John Thelwall, William Cobbett, and Richard Carlile. All were unevenly affected by empire and slavery. John Wade not only wrote his well-known *History of the Middle and Working Classes* but also served as vice president and member of the Historical Section of the Institut d'Afrique of Paris, founded "with the goal to protect, to enlighten the African race & to colonize Africa by the practical experience of missionaries."[50] As Marcus Wood has shown, William Cobbett and John Thelwall participated in discourses of Burkean parodics that inscribed the significance of race.[51]

Richard Carlile, the radical Paineite critic of organized religion, was not removed from racial assessments of political economy and his consciousness of a working class was made in correspondence with colonial gazes.[52] Carlile's papers the *Republican* and the *Lion* provide unique insights into an unruly English radical discourse transgressing colonialism in the Caribbean, British India, the American South, and beyond. This disorderly discourse addressed slavery and the constitution of blackness in one moment, and Hindu and Islamic belief in the next. These moments of address made for the awkward cohabitation of solidarities and epistemic violence.

For Carlile, black struggles in the United States and Haiti gave meaning to republicanism.[53] William Cobbett challenged Carlile's republicanism by mailing him a copy Jesse Torrey's *American Slave Trade* to point toward the hypocrisy of American republicanism. Carlile replied, "I detest and abhor the slave trade, and view the master as equally degraded with his slave. I am not one of those who think the white man a superior being to the negro. From all that I have read and witnessed, I infer that the inhabitants of Africa have mental capacities equal to the inhabitants of Asia, Europe, or America. There are shades of difference among the inhabitants of each quarter of the globe; but St. Domingo is a case in point that the negroes are a race capable of mental cultivation."[54]

Carlile's perspective further offered that there was nothing about Paine that could possibly countenance slavery. Together, these examples demonstrated radical possibilities within Paineite republican antiracism. Carlile supported the Haitian Revolution at the behest of Robert Wedderburn, whom he had met in prison, and also tried to raise money to sustain his family and promote slave revolts in Demarara.[55]

Yet these expressions of solidarity later gave way to the rhetoric of white slavery.[56] White slavery placed enslaved African Americans on the same plane as white factory workers and assessed their comparable difference through suffering. Carlile's introduction to *The Memoir of Robert Blincoe* was part of this contradictory discourse on race and suffering.[57] Blincoe's memoir, written by investigator John Brown, presented the hidden abode of production and used conventions of the slave narrative to establish the conditions of child labor in factories as "cotton-mill bondage."[58] Blincoe's life was one filled with beatings and ended with suicide. According to Brown's rendering of Blincoe's words, child factory workers were consigned "to a fate more severe than that of the West Indian slaves, who have the good fortune to serve humane owners."[59] The last words in *The Memoir* focused on the brutal violence of factory production: "No savageness in human nature, that has been on earth, has been paralleled by that which has been associated with the English cotton-spinning mills."[60] Together these reflections established the singularity of suffering produced in English cotton mills, pitted against slavery. By deploying savageness as the antithesis of republican liberty, the terminology for critique of factory exploitation turned upon the colonial need to eliminate savagery in all its form.

Carlile's preface also established the singularity of suffering within the factory even while recognizing the profound interrelation between the factory worker and the enslaved. Significantly, Carlile did not use the language "wage slavery" in his preface, but instead addressed children factory workers as "white infant-slaves."[61] Carlile further critiqued the condition of factory laborers through a staging of the emotions and thoughts of enslaved African Americans, imagining what slaves on cotton plantations would think about factory labor: "[The] cotton-slave-trade ... might have afforded a sort of sorry consolation to the Negro slaves of America, had they been informed, that their condition, in having agriculturally to raise the cotton, was not half so bad, as that of the white infant-slaves, who had to assist in the spinning of it, when brought to this country."[62] This image of terror followed capital through racialized spaces of production to differentiate suffering. The racial fantasy was especially tragic, not only because of its minstrelsy in writing, but also because it established deep economic connections between English and enslaved black labor to deny connected emancipatory projects.

Carlile continued with a critique of William Wilberforce's "black humanity," arguing that his advocacy for "slaves" was never of a "homely kind, as to embrace the region of the home-cotton-slave-trade."[63] He then asked who could read Blincoe's memoir and think that charity "should not have begun or ended at home?"[64] This insistence on the difference between home and away and what dignified life should look like in both spaces was part of a much broader conditioning of expectations within capitalism. It was central to the making of race and empire as well as the divergence between class struggle and abolition along racial lines. Such an explicitly racial division is visible in Carlile's conflation of slavery in the American South with abolition within the British Empire and his positioning of the interests of the enslaved as against the interests of the English working class.[65]

Yet it would be incomplete to see Carlile's vision of freedom as only part of the Atlantic world.[66] Unstudied but significant is Carlile's relationship to the Koran Society which, among many things, worked to publish the Quran in 1822. The ways in which he and those who worked for him addressed Hindu and Islamic religious practices were significant to articulations of freedom and Deism. Carlile's paper the *Republican* republished Orientalist literature such as Voltaire's "The Story of Bababec and the Fakirs."[67] In a letter sent to Richard Carlile, which was part of an analysis of the work of Charles-François Dupuis on the Mithraic religion, an anonymous writer noted, "The Hindus, whose religion is far more ancient than ours, have, to the present day, no greater consolation, at the last moment of their existence, than to lay hold of the tail of a *cow*, and to have themselves religiously sprinkled with its dung and urine."[68] The *Lion* republished articles such as "Pagan Origin of the Christian Religion," which had an associative logic that suggested that similarities between Krishna and Christ called into question the validity of Christianity because of its links to Hindu theology.[69] Together these perspectives were filled with both hatred and attraction in ways that remain necessary to explore in any attempt toward understanding English working class self-making.

The *Republican* also served as a venue for the critique of colonial Christianity, as one author from the Edinburgh Free-Thinkers' Zetetic Society asked, "Why do we despise the obscenity of the Hindoo and Pagan worship after adoring this? We should pull the beam out of our own eye before we attempt to take the mote out of our neighbours [*sic*] eye."[70] During the seditious libel trials of Carlile and those associated with him, a shop worker likened himself to a missionary in the colonial project of Enlightenment in England: "You offer free discussion to the Hindoo, the African, and the American Indian, then why do you fear it at home? You send Missionaries among them to impeach all that they venerate, then why do you wish to punish me for doing the same thing at home?"[71] Despite an abundance of archival material, the extent to which metropolitan working class visions of freedom corresponded with, critiqued, and engaged Orientalism and empire in relation to conceptions of freedom through racial slavery in the New World remains unknown.[72] While such moments of address may be uncommon, their presence gestures toward the complex colonial lives of the English working class.

In his *Principles of Political Economy*, the Japanese Marxist Kozo Uno argued that it was necessary to take into account the chaotic details of historical capitalism impossible to capture within a purely theoretical account.[73] Despite this long past plea, there are still very few sustained inquiries into the corresponding dynamics of capital in its "worst conceivable form." These correspondences cut across nation, the "single space" of the Atlantic, and the "unitary field" of empire, but in exactly what ways remains unclear.[74] From this perspective, the open and irreducible messiness of historical capitalism offers a generative point of departure for the antiracist and anticolonial critiques of capital. Such a critique does not necessarily begin with rescuing the past from posterity. Yet foregrounding correspondences within the transnational circuits of capital and value offers a necessary vantage point for critiquing a destructive order of global capital invested in reproducing the catastrophic present. In doing this, it is also necessary to find ourselves in good past company recognizing, as Thompson put it, that historical lives are "proto-nothing."[75]

Zach Sell *is visiting assistant professor of history at Drexel University. He is the author of* Trouble of the World: Slavery and Empire in the Age of Capital *(University of North Carolina Press).*

Notes

1. For some contours of this critique, see Cedric Robinson, *Black Marxism: The Making of the Black Radical Tradition* (London: Zed Books, 1983); Manu Goswami, "Autonomy and Comparability: Notes on the Anticolonial and the Postcolonial," *Boundaries 2* 32, no. 2 (2005): 201–225; Dipesh Chakrabarty, "Marx after Marxism: Subaltern Histories and the Question of Difference," *Polygraph* 6–7 (1993): 10–16; J. Sakai, *Settlers: The Mythology of the White Proletariat* (Chicago: Morningstar Press, 1989); Left Quarter Collective, "White Supremacist Constitution of the U.S. Empire-State: A Short Conceptual Look at the Long First Century," *Political Power and Social Theory* 20 (2009): 169–171. Marx was also profoundly insightful on slavery and colonialism; see Irfan Habib, "Introduction: Marx's Perception of India," in *Karl Marx on India*, ed. Iqbal Husain (New Delhi: Tulika Books, 2006), xix–liv; Ken Lawrence, *Karl Marx on American Slavery* (Touglaloo, MS: Freedom Information Service, 1976); Kevin B. Anderson, *Marx at the Margins: On Nationalism, Ethnicity, and Non-Western Societies* (Chicago: University of Chicago Press, 2010); Frantz Fanon, *The Wretched of the Earth* (New York: Grove Weidenfeld, 1963), 39. I am indebted to Lisa Lowe's "The Intimacies of Four Continents," in *Haunted by Empire: Geographies of Intimacy in North American History*, ed. Ann Laura Stoler (Durham, NC: Duke University Press, 2006), 191–212.
2. E. P. Thompson, *The Making of the English Working Class* (New York: Vintage Books, 2000), 13 and 249; Dipesh Chakrabarty, "Fifty Years of E. P. Thompson's *The Making of the English Working Class*," *Economic and Political Weekly* 48, no. 51 (21 December 2013): 24; Antoinette Burton, "Who Needs the Nation? Interrogating British History," *Journal of Historical Sociology* 10, no. 3 (1997): 227–248.
3. Lisa Lowe, "The Intimacies of Four Continents," in Stoler, *Haunted by Empire*, 191–212, see esp. 191.
4. Thompson, *The Making*, 191.

5. Indrajit Ray, *Bengal Industries and the British Industrial Revolution* (London: Routledge, 2011), 52–87; R. C. Dutt, *The Economic History of India under Early British Rule: From the Rise of the British Power in 1757 to the Accession of Queen Victoria in 1837*, vol. 1 (London: Kegan Paul, Trench, Trübner, 1902), 291–302; Debendra Bijoy Mitra, *Cotton Weavers of Bengal, 1757–1833* (Calcutta: Firma KLM Limited, 1978), 4, 33. Shreeram Krishnaswami, "Colonial Foundations of Western Capitalism," *Economic and Political Weekly* 27, no. 30 (25 July 1992): PE86–PE87. For dimensions of trade, see Joseph E. Inikori, "English versus Indian Cotton Textiles: The Impact of Imports on Cotton Textile Production in West Africa," in *How India Clothed the World: The World of South Asian Textiles, 1500–1850*, ed. Giorgio Riello and Tirthankar Roy (Leiden and Boston: Brill, 2009), 85–114. For Thompson's account of handloom weavers in England, see Thompson, *The Making*, 269–313.
6. H. R. Ghosal, *Economic Transition in the Bengal Presidency, 1793–1833* (Calcutta: Firma K. L. Mukhopadhyay, 1966), 30.
7. W. E. B. Du Bois, *The Negro* (New York: Henry Holt and Company, 1915), 115.
8. As Lisa Lowe has noted, this mode of comparison is a product of Weberian sociology. Lisa Lowe, "Insufficient Difference," *Ethnicities* 4, no. 3 (2005): 409–410.
9. Thompson, *The Making*, 194.
10. Karl Marx, *Pre-Capitalist Economic Formations* (New York: International Publishers, 2000), 118; Elizabeth Esch and David Roediger, "'One Symptom of Originality': Race and the Management of Labour in the History of the United States," *Historical Materialism* 17, no. 4 (2009): 4.
11. Cedric J. Robinson, "Capitalism, Marxism, and the Black Radical Tradition: An Interview with Cedric Robinson," *Perspectives on Anarchist Theory* 3, no. 1 (1999): 1, 6–8; Andrew Zimmerman, "Three Logics of Race: Theory and Exception in the Transnational History of Empire," *New Global Studies* 4, no. 1 (2010): article 6.
12. Mohinder Kumar, "Karl Marx, Andrew Ure, and the Question of Managerial Control," *Social Scientist* 12, no. 9 (1984): 64. See also W. V. Farrar, "Andrew Ure, F. R. S., and the Philosophy of Manufactures," *Notes and Records of the Royal Society of London* 27, no. 2 (1973): 299–324; Steve Edwards, "Factory and Fantasy in Andrew Ure," *Journal of Design History* 14, no. 1 (2001): 17–33; Andrew Ure, *The Philosophy of Manufactures: Or, Exploration of the Scientific, Moral, and Commercial Economy of the Factory System of Great Britain* (London: Charles Knight, 1835). E. P. Thompson's "The Moral Economy of the English Crowd" took its title from Ure's "The Moral Economy of the Factory System" in *The Philosophy of Manufactures*.
13. Andrew Ure, *The Cotton Manufacture of Great Britain*, vol. 1 (London: Charles Knight, 1836), 1. In *The Philosophy of Manufacture*, Ure also addresses the extension of the British textile industry noting that "the immense colonies ... peopled from this country" contributed to demand along with the "great fall in the prices of slaves and the productiveness of the plantations in the Valley of the Mississippi" (432).
14. On the mitigation of religious complexity within nineteenth-century colonial discourse on South Asia, see Romila Thapar, "Imagined Religious Communities? Ancient History and the Modern Search for a Hindu Identity," *Modern Asian Studies* 23, no. 2 (1989): 225–226, 209–231; Gauri Viswanathan, "Colonialism and the Construction of Hinduism," in *The Blackwell Companion to Hinduism*, ed. Gavin Flood (Malden, MA: Blackwell, 2003). See also Robert Frykenberg, "Constructions of Hinduism at the Nexus of History and Religion," *Journal of Interdisciplinary History* 23, no. 3 (1993): 523–550.
15. Ure, *Cotton Manufacture*, 12.

16. Ibid., 13. See also A Former Resident of Dacca, *A Descriptive and Historical Account of the Cotton Manufacture of Dacca, In Bengal* (London: John Mortimer, 1851); William Cooke Taylor, *The Hand Book of Silk, Cotton, and Woollen Manufactures* (London: Richard Bentley, 1843), 155.
17. Tanika Sarkar, "The Hindu Wife and the Hindu Nation: Domesticity and Nationalism in Nineteenth Century Bengal," *Studies in History* 8, no. 2 (1992): 220.
18. Edwards, "Factory and Fantasy," 19.
19. Ure, *Cotton Manufacture*, 186.
20. Ibid., v.
21. For the origins of permanent settlement, see Ranajit Guha, *A Rule of Property for Bengal: An Essay on the Idea of Permanent Settlement* (Durham, NC: Duke University Press, 1996); Manu Vimalassery, "The Wealth of Natives: Toward a Critique of Settler Colonial Political Economy," *Settler Colonial Studies* 3, nos. 3–4 (2013): 295–310.
22. William Bentinck, "Minute of the Governor-General," 30 May 1829, 274–280. In *East India Company's Affairs Report and General Index*, vol. VIII, 1831–32. Hereafter cited as "Minute."
23. Ibid., 275.
24. Transformations in indigo cultivation were significant to Bentinck's vision of reworking colonial India into a colony existing especially for the production of raw materials. See Prakash Kumar, *Indigo Plantations and Science in Colonial India* (Cambridge: Cambridge University Press, 2012), 77–81.
25. Ibid., 277.
26. Aziz Rana, *Two Faces of American Freedom* (Cambridge, MA: Harvard University Press, 2010), 65–67.
27. On Bentinck's colonial economics, see John Rosselli, *Lord William Bentinck: The Making of a Liberal Imperialist, 1774–1839* (Delhi: Thomson Press [India] Limited, 1974), 272–325; Ranajit Guha, *Dominance without Hegemony: History and Power in Colonial India* (Cambridge, MA: Harvard University Press, 1997), 33–34.
28. Bentinck, "Minute," 278.
29. John Locke, *Two Treatises of Government*, ed. Peter Laslett (Cambridge: Cambridge University Press, 1988), 294, 287; Rana, *Two Faces*, 34; Barbara Arneil, "The Wild Indian's Venison: Locke's Theory of Property and English Colonialism in America," *Political Studies* 44, no. 1 (1996): 60–74.
30. On surplus population, see Michael McIntyre, "Race, Surplus Population and the Marxist Theory of Imperialism," *Antipode* 43, no. 5 (2011): 1439–1515.
31. On the orientations of empire and settler capitalism, see Jodi A. Byrd, "Follow the Typical Signs: Settler Sovereignty and Its Discontents," *Settler Colonial Studies* 4, no. 2 (2013): 2–4.
32. Viswanathan, "Colonialism and the Construction of Hinduism."
33. Bentinck, "Minute," 277.
34. Ibid.
35. Arnold, "Agriculture and 'Improvement'," 510.
36. "14 June 1832." Manuscript Minutes of the Agricultural and Horticultural Society of India. Agricultural and Horticultural Society of India, Kolkata.
37. Peter L. Rousseau, "Jacksonian Monetary Policy, Specie Flows, and the Panic of 1837," *Journal of Economic History* 62, no. 2 (2002): 457–488; Jessica M. Lepler, "1837: Anatomy of a Panic" (PhD diss., Brandeis University, 2008); Dennis East, "The New York and Mississippi Land Company and the Panic of 1837," *Journal of*

Mississippi History 33, no. 4 (1971): 299–331; Clara Sue Kidwell, *Choctaws and Missionaries in Mississippi, 1818–1918* (Norman: University of Oklahoma Press, 1995), 166–167; Edwin Arthur Miles, *Jacksonian Democracy in Mississippi* (Chapel Hill: University of North Carolina Press, 1960), 133–134.

38. James Hammond, *Anniversary Oration of the State Agricultural Society of South Carolina* (Columbia, SC: A. S. Johnston, 1841), 8.
39. Ibid., 6.
40. Ibid., 8.
41. Ibid., 9. See also David Roediger and Elizabeth Esch, *The Production of Difference* (Oxford: Oxford University Press, 2012), 19–39.
42. Hammond, *Anniversary Oration*, 12.
43. On this capacity, see Walter Johnson, *River of Dark Dreams: Slavery and Empire in the Cotton Kingdom* (Cambridge, MA: Harvard University Press, 2013).
44. James Oakes, "The Peculiar Fate of the Bourgeois Critique of Slavery," in *Slavery and the American South*, ed. Winthrop D. Jordan (Jackson: University of Mississippi Press, 2003), 44–45.
45. W. E. B. Du Bois, *The World and Africa* (New York: International Publishers, 1965).
46. Thompson, *The Making*, 194.
47. Ibid., 806. See also Peter Linebaugh and Marcus Rediker, *The Many-Headed Hydra* (Boston: New Beacon Press, 2000), 287–326; Iain McCalman, "Anti-Slavery and Ultra-Radicalism in Early Nineteenth-Century England: The Case of Robert Wedderburn," *Slavery and Abolition* 7, no. 2 (1986): 99–117; Paul Gilroy, *The Black Atlantic: Modernity and Double Consciousness* (London and New York: Verso, 1993), 12.
48. James Walvin, "The Impact of Slavery on British Radical Politics: 1787–1838," *Annals of the New York Academy of Sciences* 292, no. 1 (1977): 345; Peter Linebaugh, "All the Atlantic Mountains Shook," *Labour/Le Travail* 10 (1982): 87–121; Iain McCalman, "Anti-Slavery and Ultra-Radicalism."
49. Thompson, *The Making*, 711–832.
50. "*Institut d'Afrique*," *The Correspondence of William Henry Fox Talbot*, 1 April 1840, accessed 1 January 2015, http://foxtalbot.dmu.ac.uk/letters/transcriptName.php?bcode=Talb-WH&pageNumber=3852&pageTotal=10045&referringPage=192; John Wade, *History of the English Working and Middle Classes* (London: Effingham Wilson, 1833).
51. Marcus Wood, "William Cobbett, John Thelwall, Radicalism, Racism and Slavery: A Study in Burkean Parodics," *Romanticism on the Net* 15 (1999): http://www.erudit.org/revue/ron/1999/v/n15/005873ar.html.
52. Thompson, *The Making*, 762–768; Angela Keane, "Richard Carlile's Working Women: Selling Books, Politics, Sex, and *The Republican*," *Literature & History* 15, no. 2 (2006): 20–33.
53. Richard Carlile, "To the Republicans of the Island of Great Britain," *Republican* 5, no. 3 (1822): 65–71.
54. Ibid., 67.
55. McCalman, "Anti-Slavery and Ultra-Radicalism," 113.
56. Gunther Peck, "White Slavery and Whiteness: A Transnational View of the Sources of Working-Class Radicalism and Racism," *Labor: Studies in Working-Class History of the Americas* 1, no. 2 (2004): 41–63; David Roediger, *The Wages of Whiteness: Race and the Making of the American Working Class*, 65–87; Joseph Persky, "Wage Slavery," *History of Political Economy* 30, no. 4 (1998): 627–650.

57. Thompson, *The Making,* 94. The memoir is serialized in the *Lion* 1, nos. 4–8, 119–128; 145–158; 181–192; 214–224; 248–256. For Carlile's preface, see the *Lion* 1, no. 5 (1 February 1828): 145–146.
58. 1, no. 4 (1828): 119. The memoir, with Carlile's preface, was republished: John Brown, *A Memoir of Robert Blincoe, an Orphan Boy* (Manchester: J. Doherty, 1832).
59. *Lion* 1, no. 4 (1828): 126.
60. *Lion* 1, no. 8 (1828): 256.
61. *Lion* 1, no. 5 (1828): 145.
62. Ibid.
63. Ibid.
64. Ibid.
65. Roediger, *Wages of Whiteness,* 66.
66. Joel Wiener, *Radicalism and Freethought in Nineteenth-Century Britain: The Life of Richard Carlile* (Westport, CT: Greenwood Press, 1983). As Wiener notes, Carlile was influenced by William Jones's *Asiatic Researches.*
67. Voltaire, "The Story of Bababec and the Fakirs," *Republican* 13, no. 23 (1826): 711–713.
68. Fellow Citizen, "To Richard Carlile, Dorchester Gaol: Continuation of an Analysis of Dupuis," *Republican* 10, no. 16 (1824): 499. Letter dated 3 August 1824.
69. "Pagan Origin of the Christian Religion," *Lion* 2, no. 5 (1828): 142–144. From the *New York Correspondent.* See also Wiener, *Radicalism,* 152.
70. R. A., "A Critical Enquiry into the Harmony of the Books of Matthew, Mark, Luke, and John," *Republican* 5, no. 10 (1822): 310.
71. *Report of the Trial of Humphrey Boyle* (London: R. Carlile [published at Koran Society's office], 1822), 19.
72. Lowe, "Intimacies," 191–212.
73. Kozo Uno, *Principles of Political Economy: Theory of a Purely Capitalist Society* (Sussex: Harvester, 1980).
74. Walter Johnson, "The Pedestal and the Veil: Rethinking the Capitalism/ Slavery Question," *Journal of the Early Republic* 24, no. 2 (2004): 304; Bernard Cohn, *Colonialism and Its Forms of Knowledge: The British in India* (Princeton, NJ: Princeton University Press, 1996).
75. E. P. Thompson, *Customs in Common: Studies in Traditional Popular Culture* (New York: Penguin Books, 1993), 320; David Roediger, "'Even Marxism': Reflections on Class, Listening and U.S. Labor History" (Unpublished Paper, 1994).

Chapter 5

Race, Antiracism, and the Place of Blackness in the Making and Remaking of the English Working Class

Caroline Bressey

Many talks and papers commemorating the fiftieth anniversary of E. P. Thompson's *The Making of the English Working Class* reflect on the influence of the book—how historians read it as undergraduate or graduate scholars and found an inspirational narrative and methodological process that opened new directions of interpretation and research. The absences—particularly around the histories of women—have been well documented. For many it was Thompson's lack of focus on gender, empire, and laborers such as factory workers that stimulated their own research to recover "new worlds of political activity in the streets and taverns of towns and cities across America, France, Italy, India";[1] it is the absence of "black history" in *The Making* that is the focus of my reflections here. The black presence in Britain was and remains marginalized in the retelling of the Isles' history in both scholarly and popular form. Its persistent absence illustrates the complex politics of belonging in historical narratives and the reluctance of many to examine the intersections of class and race and gender in political activism, particularly antiracist activism in Britain.

In this article I revisit some of the sources used by Thompson in *The Making* to draw attention to histories of the black presence within them. These, I argue, suggest a greater overlapping of race and class in the actions and ideals of some of the activists present in *The Making,* and as such there is still much work to be done in order to unpack the many layers of political work undertaken by characters in and beyond the pages of *The Making.* Thompson's narrative is undoubtedly an immense achievement and it can seem churlish to list the material that is clearly missing—how many more pages would one really wish it to be? But it is undoubtedly true that a rewriting of the history of the English working class that gave equal weight to the experiences and roles of women and "race" in the making of the English working class would result in a different narrative.

Historical Geographies of the Black Presence in Britain

To be fair to Thompson, a historian approaching this material when he was writing would have not been well supported by their peers. There was very little on the history of black people in Britain available. Kathleen Chater's research indicates that M. Dorothy George was the first modern historian to mention the historical presence of black people in her research of London in the eighteenth century published in 1925.[2] In a chapter on immigrants and emigrants, George looks at Jewish and Irish communities alongside lascars who came to London through the networks of the East India Company and "negroes in London."[3] In the same chapter George reflects that few up to that date had commented on the "great number" of black people in the city. George found black residents in the archives of the courts of the Old Bailey, in newspapers and runaway notices, and in legal cases, among them that of Katherine Aucker, a black woman who, in 1690, petitioned to be discharged from her absentee master.[4] George saw London's eighteenth-century black presence as made up of a people who were "immigrants a class apart," but who also led complex working lives.[5] They did not live in ethnically segregated ghettos and, while many experienced enslavement, there were reports of black apprentices who were "apparently as free as other apprentices," though, as George acknowledged, this was "perhaps not saying much."[6] George's *London Life in the Eighteenth Century* is referenced in *The Making,* while Kenneth Little's *Negroes in Britain* is not.[7] Published in 1948, Little's work is largely a survey of the black community in Cardiff, but it does contain a brief history of the presence of black people in Britain from 1600 to 1948.[8] Peter Fryer's *Staying Power,* a seminal text on the history of "Black People" (meaning, in the context of the political language of Britain at the time, people of both African and Asian descent) would not be published until 1984.[9]

It is not that race is entirely absent from *The Making*. There is a reference, for example, to the Jamaican born William Davidson, who was one of five men executed for their role in the Cato Street Conspiracy, on 1 May 1820, in the last public decapitation in England. Born in Jamaica in 1786, Davidson was sent across the Atlantic to be educated in Edinburgh. After some time press-ganged into the Navy, studying in Aberdeen and the failure of his business in Birmingham, Davidson settled in London working again as a cabinet maker in south London, living with his wife and four stepsons near the old Lord's Cricket Ground. Together he and his wife Sarah had two more sons. Peter Fryer describes Davidson's local popularity and that, following his membership of the Marylebone Union Reading Society—where members met regularly to read radical newspapers—he began holding meetings of up to eighteen people at his home. His work would earn him a place on a list of thirty-three leading reformers compiled from reports for the home secretary in October 1819.[10] Through a police spy and provocateur George Edwards, Davidson was introduced to Arthur Thistlewood's radical group; Davidson became secretary of the shoemakers' trade union and chaired some of the group's meetings. Here, the police provocateur suggested they carry out violent attacks against the government, encouraging their outrage against the Peterloo massacre. Richard Carlile, who appears throughout *The Making*, wrote to Sarah following Davidson's execution, apologizing for his mistaken belief that Davidson, not Edwards, had been the government informant. In his public letter of apology he wrote, "Be assured that the heroic manner in which your husband and his companions met their fate, will in a few years, perhaps in a few months, stamp their names as patriots, and men who had nothing but their country's weal at heart. I flatter myself as your children grow up, they will find that the fate of their father will rather procure them respect and admiration than its reverse."[11]

References to race in a broad sense do occur earlier in Thompson's narrative than the Cato Street Conspiracy. In the preface Thompson acknowledges that he is focusing on the English to the exclusion of the Scottish and Welsh. He argues that he does this not out of chauvinism but out of respect, what we could now perhaps read as a sensitive acknowledgement of the geopolitics of whiteness. Thompson also reflects briefly on "The white slaves [who] left our shores for the American plantations and later for Van Diemen's Land, while Bristol and Liverpool were enriched with the profits of black slavery."[12] But while this reference to white slaves leaving and profits arriving has a persuasive literary flow, its conflation of white indentured labor and prison transportation with chattel slavery is problematic. It also reveals Thompson's inaccurate assumption of the whiteness of those pioneer prisoners sent to Australia, which has been made increasingly visible by historians such as Ian Duffield and Cassandra Pybus. Their research can now be used by scholars who have access to a wealth of digital archive resources, such as the Old Bailey online.[13] In a 1987 paper exploring "aspects of the Black convict contribution to resistance patterns during the transportation era in Eastern Australia," Ian Duffield traced the experiences of John Goff, a seaman born on the Isle of Wight in about 1792.[14] Sentenced to transportation for fourteen years in 1814 in the Devon Assizes, Duffield argues that Goff's "subversive attachment to liberty in Australia, and his refusal to be submissive as a convict" are important and suggestive of Goff's agency in the context of a coming together of working-class rights and the emancipation struggle of black people in an age of slavery.[15] In September 1826 Goff led an uprising on Norfolk Island that was followed by a mass escape of one-third of the convicts; for his role in the death of Corporal Robert Wilson during the violence Goff was sentenced to hang and he was executed in Sydney on 24 September 1827.

The first mention of a black man does not occur until page 769 (in my edition of *The Making*), and there are no black women at all, though there was an opportunity in the context of Colonel Edward Despard.[16] Having served his country for thirty years Despard was found guilty of a conspiracy against the state and was hanged in February 1803. Increasingly interested in radical politics and the cause of Irish independence, in the 1790s the Irish born Despard joined the London Corresponding Society (LCS)—a group of shopkeepers, mechanics, and tradesmen focused on political reform who came together in 1792—and the United Irishmen and United Englishmen in London. Thompson explains that Despard was arrested during the suspension of habeas corpus between 1798 and 1800; following his release in 1800 he was again arrested in November 1802, at the Oakley Arms in Lambeth, south London, in the company of men deemed to be part of his revolutionary conspiracy. Given his link to the LCS and revolutionary politics it is not surprising that Despard is mentioned several times in *The Making*. Thompson argues that "the Despard affair must be seen as an incident of real significance in British political history," but Despard's black wife, Catherine Despard is not considered as a part of that political moment.[17] It is Linebaugh and Reddiker's account of the revolutionary Atlantic, which emphasizes its multiethnic history, that draws attention to Catherine's political contribution to the making of English working class politics.[18] Catherine accompanied her husband from central America to England in 1790, and Linebaugh and Reddiker illustrate the important lobbying role she played not only in defense of her husband, but for prisoners' rights more broadly. They reconfigure the "Despard affair" as a partnership between Catherine and Edward, a union that "may stand for a new cycle of rebellion that began in the 1790s, from which emerged not only the race and class themes in the age of revolution but also a new definition of the human race."[19]

Thompson's assumptions about the whiteness of fleets of transportees sent to Australia are closely connected to the presumed whiteness of the English working class at home. Though an acknowledgement of the profits of black labor coming to British shores is clearly made in *The Making*, enslaved black men and women workers themselves remain off shore, and there is no consideration given to how a man such as William Davidson—the son of a black woman and Jamaica's attorney general—who studied in Scotland and bought a house in Birmingham where he set up trade as a cabinet maker, arrived at the gallows with his fellow Cato Street conspirators. The conflation of chattel slavery to that of indentured laborers and prisoners is uncomfortable, but the reference in this context to North America, the West Indies, and Australia gives no thought to the communities who lived on those lands before the arrival of the English and their capitalist adventurers, and so another strand of empire, the oppression of indigenous people and their complex relationship to the formation of the English working class, is also avoided.

The reluctance of the British Left to consider the presence of black workers or include the contribution of black activists to formations of radical politics in Britain has been highlighted most recently by David Featherstone through his work on *Solidarity*.[20] Featherstone has previously researched the hidden histories and geographies of political solidarity through the London Corresponding Society, an organization that appears on the first page of *The Making*.[21] The introduction of the LCS at the front of Thompson's narrative could have been a tool to underscore the multiplicity of concerns that at least some working people had in the 1790s. When including the links of the LCS to black radicals it can be more clearly seen that, as Fryer argued, for some working class radicals "black and white freedom were two sides of one coin."[22] The link between the LCS and the former slave Olaudah Equiano are key to an understanding of their position.

Olaudah Equiano was a friend of Thomas Hardy, the first secretary of the LCS.[23] Equiano stayed with Hardy and his wife Lydia at their home in London while he was working on the manuscript for a new edition of his autobiography, *The Interesting Narrative of Olaudah Equiano, or Gustavas Vassa, The African*, first published in 1789.[24] Between 1789 and 1794 Equiano toured England, Scotland, Wales, and Ireland to promote his *Interesting Narrative* in what John Bugg calls "the first modern-style author tour in British history."[25] Equiano spent most of 1791 and 1792 visiting towns and cities such as Derby, Nottingham, Halifax, and Sheffield—all of them points on *The Making*'s geopolitical map—selling his book and drumming up support for the abolition movement. Bugg reflects that the cultural significance of Equiano's tour has been largely ignored probably because it ended in the summer 1794, when Equiano found himself caught up in the arrests of members of the LCS in May. Bugg's suggestion builds upon Vincent Carretta's observation that, among the list of subscribers for the fifth and later editions of Equiano's *Narrative*, the names of Thomas Hardy and George Walne, Hardy's brother-in-law and organizer of the LCS, as well as the formerly enslaved radical Quobna Ottobah Cugoano, disappeared.[26] During his book tours Equiano acted like an agent for the LCS, passing on to Hardy the names and addresses of abolitionists whom he met that thought would be sympathetic to the cause of the LCS.[27] Among the evidence gathered by the state during the repression of the movement in 1794 was a letter from Equiano to Hardy.[28] The ninth and final edition of Equiano's *Narrative* was published in 1794. Though Hardy was acquitted in November following his arrest in May of that year, both Bugg and Carretta speculate that the clampdown on the activism of the LCS may explain Equiano's apparent public silence after 1794.

Fryer illustrates that combining demands for black and white freedom were not only to be found among members of the LCS. He reports that at Sheffield's largest demonstration of workers in April 1794—a city Equiano had visited in 1790 and perhaps also in 1792—a thousand artisan cutlers supported a unanimous resolution for the emancipation of enslaved Africans as well as an end to the slave trade.[29] For Hardy and his wife, Lydia, who was involved in the domestic sugar boycott, the link between black and white workers' rights was clear.[30] In the inaugural letter of the LCS addressed to the Rev. Mr. Henry Bryant of Sheffield in March 1792 to introduce him to the work and aims of the LCS, Hardy wrote,

> I hope you will pardon that freedom which I take in troubling you with the following sentiments; nothing but the importance of the business could have induced me to address one who is an entire stranger to me, except only by *report*. Hearing from my friend, Gustavus Vassa, the African, who is now writing memoirs of his life in my house, that you are a zealous friend to the abolition of that cursed traffic, the Slave Trade, I infer, from that circumstance, *that you are a zealous friend to freedom on the broad basis of the RIGHTS OF MAN*. I am fully persuaded that there is no man, who is, from principle, an advocate for the liberty of the black man, but will zealously support the rights of the white man, and vice versa.[31]

Thompson surely read Thomas Hardy's memoir closely, but mention of "Gustavas Vassa, the African" in a key document of the LCS did not seem to pique his curiosity. Featherstone argues that, on greater reflection, the LCS can be seen to have been "shaped by practices where it makes little sense to make such a rigid distinction between the 'local' and the 'universal'."[32] William Davidson and Equiano embodied these geographies and evoked them in their political campaigns; in his campaign to galvanize an international campaign against slavery, Equiano described himself as a "citizen of the world."[33] Equiano, Davidson, and the Hardys understood only too well the inherent geographies of inequality that produced the sugar that flowed "through English blood and rotted English teeth."[34]

For researchers particularly interested in why race became such a key stratification of working class politics, organizations such as the LCS provide an opportunity to attempt to unpack why some protests within working class organizations sought to embrace a diverse and international foundation for working class solidarity, and why others did not. An unpacking of their networks of solidarity may also reveal more about the ability of some working class organizations to establish themselves and why others came under particular scrutiny at particular times. One hypothesis is that Equiano could travel more freely than members of the LCS because of his antislavery work, a cause sympathetically viewed by many at the time. Following from this, it is also possible that the LCS could not be tolerated by the State because it advocated freedoms not only for an English working class, but a working people that included the enslaved on the plantations of Britain's empire. There may also be more to uncover around the intersections of class solidarity and ideals of racial equality during the period. Josiah Wedgwood would become famous for the "Am I not a Man and a Brother" antislavery motif designed and produced by his pottery company, but as Thompson notes, Wedgwood and other industrialists linked with the abolition campaign did not actively link with Hardy and the LCS, while Equiano and perhaps other leading black activists did. How race was understood in activist imaginations is surely a key to understanding these different pathways to solidarity.

Attempting to unpack these aspects of labor politics should not be marginal to a rethinking of a Thompsonian formulation of the making of the English working class. Certainly such ideas were not marginal to the concerns of Equiano or the Sons of Africa, the London based collective of which he was a part, or for white activists such as the Hardys, the LCS, or later antiracist activists like the Quaker Catherine Impey and her colleague Celestine Edwards. Entangled in these narratives of labor politics are the complexities around the growth of class consciousness that Thompson identifies as an identity of interests between diverse groups of working people and against the interest of other classes. There are also the complexities of whiteness, an identity that for some would override class interests. For others whose skin marked them as black, racism made it exceedingly difficult for them to maintain class based solidarities. To ignore these interclass conflicts belies the complexities of solidarity and does not help us understand as well as we might why antiracism failed to become a core part of the working class intellectual tradition in England, or why the working class movement split between those who held on to a universal notion of equality and those who, in the nineteenth century and following World War I, asserted and reasserted nationalistically and ethnically bounded ideas of equality. Nor does it help us capture how the "optimistic imaginaries" of activists, such as those working with Catherine Impey's anticaste movement, sought to understand and overcome class competition in the context of the deeply radicalized and racist world of the late nineteenth century.[35]

Race, Class, and Caste

In 1885 Catherine Impey wrote an essay on "Some Diverse Views on Social Equality" for the *Village Album* in which she examined what she called the "right relations" between "rich and poor, or the cultured and the uncultured" in America, England, and around the world.[36] Impey presented her audience with an exploratory discussion of "social rights" and "civil rights" within a conception of "human rights." These ideas of rights in the context of political reform informed her writing and the editorial voice of her monthly periodical *Anti-Caste.* From this small town in rural Somerset Impey challenged racial prejudice in the British Empire and the United States and, beginning in March 1888, edited and distributed copies of *Anti-Caste,* possibly Britain's first antiracist periodical. She hoped *Anti-Caste*'s community of readers would become the foundation for an international antiracist movement that would unite "blacks and whites and Indians, Africans, Americans and Europeans" to work "for the emancipation of all men everywhere from disabilities imposed on the ground of colour or race."[37] In what can now be read as an early contribution to ideas of intersectionality, Impey identified issues of racial prejudice to be more difficult to overcome than those of class alone, arguing that in the United States questions of rights and equality were complicated by issues "about differences of race."[38] She similarly observed that in South Africa, processes of inequality and oppression were dominated by "class feeling emphasised by differences of colour."[39] For Impey racial prejudice was produced and maintained by white people through social and economic systems of oppression. Over the six years of its publication, *Anti-Caste* sought to provide a space in which these systems of oppression could be exposed, and those oppressed by the inequalities of racial prejudice could speak to an audience at the heart of empire and to each other.[40]

To create the content for *Anti-Caste* Impey relied on local news written and edited by African, African American, and Indian journalists and *Anti-Caste* readers whom she described as her "co-workers."[41] Though she attempted to draw together an internationalized content for *Anti-Caste,* it was the divisive and at times extremely violent racism operating in the United States that was most often reported. This reflected Impey's personal connections to American civil rights workers, including Frederick Douglass, T. Thomas Fortune, and Albion Tourgée. *Anti-Caste*'s most high profile work came with the collaboration of Catherine Impey and the African American feminist and activist Ida B. Wells during their anti-lynching campaigns in 1893 and 1894. But although the "American Question" dominated the first issue of *Anti-Caste,* within six months examples of discrimination and injustices in Australia, Brazil, Canada, India, and colonies in the Caribbean and Africa had also been reported. The number of regular readers *Anti-Caste* attracted did not amount to a large group. The subscriber list for *Anti-Caste* probably never reached more than 350 households at its peak, though the distribution of free copies boosted circulation towards, and sometimes beyond, 3,500 each month. Free copies particularly targeted spaces accessible to working class readers such as YMCA reading rooms in America and free public libraries in Britain. Over its lifetime the periodical produced a reading community of progressive radicals: vegetarians, early feminists, early socialists, pacifists, and international students based in Britain, as well as antislavery campaigners. International readers were present from the outset either as subscribers or, like the radical African American journalist T. Thomas Fortune, they were part of the editorial exchange network that provided *Anti-Caste* with its often challenging content. International subscribers were usually located in the United States, but the periodical also had readers in Africa and the Caribbean.

Segregation, lynching, legal injustice, and colonial expansion were all themes covered in *Anti-Caste*. Reporting on the racialized exploitation of workers in the Empire and the United States proved an effective way for *Anti-Caste* to demonstrate the everyday forms of racism experienced by ordinary people. The exploitation of "native" workers in southern Africa, the abuse of Chinese workers in the United States and Australia, as well as the deplorable conditions of the Kanaka (Pacific Island workers) on the sugar plantations of Queensland all featured in issues of *Anti-Caste*.[42] The harsh realities of working life on tea plantations were an aspect underpinning consumer culture in England that *Anti-Caste* sought to expose through the republication of details from a report on the imprisonment of an assistant manager of an Assam tea plantation for his "assault on coolies" and other injustices faced by the plantation workers. To bring the unjust treatment of the tea plantation workers home to her readers, Impey compared their troubles to those of factory workers in Britain. What would readers say, she asked, if there were a factory in England where half, or even a quarter of the workers died every year; what would they say to a government that forced employees to fulfill the full term of a contract which they had entered into while they were ignorant of the nature of the work they were to undertake?[43]

In the summer of 1893, after six years as editor and proprietor, Impey transferred the editorship of the periodical to Celestine Edwards, probably Britain's first black editor. Under his tenure the paper expanded and was renamed *Fraternity*, and he maintained a relentless criticism of racial prejudice and the exploitation of the people of color throughout the world. Unlike many of his African American peers, Edwards was not a trained journalist. As a boy he had left the Caribbean as a stowaway on a French ship and began his life as a seaman. In 1873 he had found himself in New York, though by 1875 he had moved on to San Francisco where he decided to try and make a life on land. Narrowly missing being shot during a fight caused Edwards to reflect on his life in America and he went back to sea. Around 1878 Edwards found himself at Hull, and from there he moved on to Edinburgh where he lived for about two years.[44] By the time of England's 1891 census he was living in East London and was a popular and active speaker on aspects of Christianity and temperance.[45] In 1893 Edwards was among the speakers addressing a Trade Union march in Portsmouth. The three thousand demonstrators included members of the Boilermakers' Society, the General Labourers' Amalgamated Union, coppersmiths, bricklayers, joiners, plasters, dockers, railway workers, stone masons, iron founders, and insurance agents. Speaking to the crowd, Edwards proposed a motion for the meeting to push for the improved conditions of workers and the placement of labor representatives on all local governing bodies. He encouraged the unionists to better educate themselves by meeting together in clubrooms so they could discuss "the vital questions which lay at the very root of happiness and peace." [46] He also argued that only once workers had settled their petty differences could they conduct a peaceful war against the capitalists.

Edwards undertook his speaking tours alongside the editorship of *Fraternity.* Like *Anti-Caste,* the paper strived to provide its readers with international reports, but it also maintained a high profile on lynchings in the United States. They illustrated only too well the regular column of "Things as they are and should not be." The column covered the social and economic disadvantages placed on black people, especially Americans, from the proposed racial segregation of tax allocations in Alabama to the pervasive attempts to keep black Americans from the ballot box.[47] Edwards juxtaposed these reports of inequality, oppression, and murder with columns in which more heartening stories were shared, reporting examples of everyday heroism and conviviality in America and Britain. The columns also celebrated the successes of people of color, primarily heralding stories of "Coloured Inventors," scientists, and "Good Business Men" mainly from North America, where African American newspapers collected and reported on the progress of their communities and where the personal achievements of individuals were closely linked to community politics. Edwards had a similar editorial goal, to argue for the integration of black individuals into all levels of society, but this meant that interconnecting issues of class and race within black communities were not often directly challenged in *Fraternity.* For example, in November 1893 *Fraternity* celebrated the sacking of a group of white waiters at the Avenue Hotel in St Louis following their protest against a black waiter being placed in their charge; all were replaced by black workers.[48] Given the injustices faced by black people in so many realms of employment it is not surprising *Fraternity* celebrated the white workers' failure on this occasion, but it was an indication of how successfully racism played its role in undermining a politics of solidarity between black and white workers against their employers. It also reflected the problematic outcomes of segregation present in Frederick Douglass's warnings in an earlier letter to *Anti-Caste* in which he had argued that black communities who supported segregated education were shortsighted. Like Equiano and the LCS, Douglass argued that true freedom would only be realized with a fundamental remaking of a united and integrated society.[49] Despite the potential for antiracist class politics, by the end of the nineteenth century the interests of white workers in the United States and across the British Empire became solidified within narratives of whiteness.[50] This was, as historians have highlighted, an identity that was not forced on workers but one that many demanded.[51]

Though neither born before Thompson's empirical cut-off date of the 1830s, nor working class, Catherine Impey's activism reflects the many complexities inherent in the making of successful solidarities. For both Edwards and Impey, working on antiracist activism meant acknowledging that the politics of labor and work was complexly overlaid with prejudices that operated in materially different ways in different, though connected, places. As an activist and a woman Impey's work is certainly part of a body of historical scholarship that was inspired by Thompson's emphasis on examining "history from below." Her rural base in Street, where she lived for her entire life, places an interesting geographical perspective on the place from which radical movements might emerge—and is a rebuff to those who criticize Thompson's decision to halt his examination before the firm establishment of a factory workforce and his subsequent emphasis on rural radicalism.[52] As an editor and activist Impey was undoubtedly a middle class worker. She was also, through her family's farm, an employer of laborers, and through *Anti-Caste* an employer of artisans (her printers John Whitby and Son in Bridgwater, Somerset). Her father Robert Impey was remembered for his commitment to modernizing agricultural technology that also brought him into conflict with local workers. But though Impey was middle class, *Anti-Caste* was not a wholly middle class enterprise.[53] Celestine Edwards, who originated from the Caribbean and worked as a seaman and laborer before his work as an editor, certainly was not. Although difficult to uncover, evidence of the anticaste movement's working class component is present. One example was made public via a letter to Edwards from Ms J. Simons. She wrote to Edwards on behalf of her band of Christian "workwomen" who discussed the content of *Fraternity* with their Sunday school teacher. The group of women committed to save one penny a week and to send the collected sum to Edwards once a month. They hoped Edwards would accept their contribution and that their actions would inspire others to support the cause.[54]

Thompson could not rescue everyone from the "enormous condescension of posterity," and there is still a large amount of rescue work to be done on the histories of women and the histories of race and antiracist activism in Britain. The dynamic processes of race and formations of racism were place specific, but how people sought to challenge the consequences of racism could and did cut across national boundaries, and class, as in the collaboration between Impey, Edwards, and their anticaste collective. Such cross cutting did not reflect an absence of national or class based concerns, but were part of the complex matrix activists formed, far beyond as well as within the national borders of "the English." Those working for political reform among the eighteenth-century English working class, including Olaudah Equiano and his colleagues who made up the Sons of Africa, Catherine Despard, Thomas and Lydia Hardy, and William Davidson, held ideals with a far greater "optimistic imaginary" than they are given credit for in *The Making*. The extent of their activist networks alongside those of later communities, such as Impey and Edwards' *Anti-Caste* readers, are among many historical narratives still waiting to be given due consideration.

Caroline Bressey is a Reader in Cultural and Historical Geography in the Department of Geography, University College London. Her research focuses on recovering the social lives and understandings of race and racism experienced by those who were a part of the black presence in Victorian Britain, particularly working-class London. Drawing together geographies of international reading communities, women's activism and radical 'anti-caste' politics in nineteenth century Britain, her book Empire, Race and the politics of Anti-Caste *was awarded the Women's History Network Book Prize in 2014 and the Colby Book Prize in 2015.*

Notes

1. Kathleen Wilson, "Class and Condescension," *History Workshop Journal* 76, no. 1 (2013): 251–255, 252.
2. M. Dorothy George, *London Life in the Eighteenth Century* (London: Kegan Paul, 1925); Kathleen Chater, "Making History: Black British History," accessed 30 September 2014, www.history.ac.uk/makinghistory/resources/articles/black_history.html#2.
3. George, *London Life in the Eighteenth Century,* 184.
4. A transcript of the record for Auker's case can be seen online at the UK National Archives website, accessed 30 September 2014, http://www.nationalarchives.gov.uk/pathways/blackhistory/rights/slave_free.htm.
5. George, *London Life in the Eighteenth Century,* 134.
6. Ibid., 137.
7. See "Artisans and Others," Thompson, *The Making.*
8. Kenneth Little, *Negroes in Britain: A Study of Racial Relations in English Society* (London: Kegan Paul, 1948).
9. Peter Fryer, *Staying Power: The History of Black People in Britain* (London: Pluto, 1984). On Fryer, see Terry Brotherstone, "Obituary: Peter Fryer, Communist Journalist Who Told the Truth about Hungary 1956," *Guardian* (3 November 2006).
10. This biographical information on Davidson comes from Fryer, *Staying Power,* 214–220. Fryer notes that the Jamaican born radical Robert Wedderburn was also on this list.
11. Cited in Fryer, *Staying Power,* 220.
12. Thompson, *The Making,* 66.
13. Cassandra Pybus, *Black Founders: The Unknown Story of Australia's First Black Settlers* (Sydney: University of New South Wales Press, 2006). The Proceedings of the Old Baily online database is available at www.oldbaileyonline.org.
14. Ian Duffield, "The Life and Death of 'Black Goff': Aspects of the Black Convict Contribution to Resistance Patterns during the Transportation Era in Eastern Australia," *Australian Journal of Politics and History* 33, no. 1 (1987): 30–44.
15. Ibid., 32.
16. Thompson, *The Making;* Despard is named Colonel Edmund Despard in *The Making.*
17. Thompson, *The Making,* 526.
18. Peter Leinbaugh and Marcus Reddiker, *The Many-Headed Hydra: The Hidden History of the Revolutionary Atlantic* (London: Verso, 2000).
19. Ibid., 254.

20. David Featherstone, *Solidarity: Hidden Histories and Geographies of Internationalism* (London: Zed Books, 2012).
21. David Featherstone, *Resistance, Space and Political Identities: The Making of Counter-Global Networks* (Oxford: Blackwell, 2008).
22. Fryer, *Staying Power*, 106.
23. David Featherstone, "Contested Relationalities of Political Activism: The Democratic Spatial Practices of the London Corresponding Society," *Cultural Dynamics* 22 (2010): 87–104.
24. Vincent Carretta, *Equiano, The African: Biography of a Self-Made Man* (Athens: University of Georgia Press, 2005).
25. John Bugg, "The Other Interesting Narrative: Olaudah Equiano's Public Book Tour," *PMLA* 121, no. 5 (2006): 1424–1442, 1424.
26. Carretta, *Equiano, The African*.
27. Fryer, *Staying Power*.
28. Bugg, "The Other Interesting Narrative."
29. Carretta, *Equiano, The African*; Fryer, *Staying Power*, 211.
30. On Lydia Hardy and women's involvement in the sugar boycott, see Clare Midgley, *Women Against Slavery: The British Campaigns, 1780–1870* (London and New York: Routledge, 1992).
31. Thomas Hardy to Rev Mr Bryant of Sheffield 8 March 1792, reprinted in *Memoir of Thomas Hardy* (London: James Ridgway, 1832), 14–15. In his memoir Hardy noted that he republished the letter because during his trial the Attorney General "lamented very much—he is good at lamentations—that he has no possession of it" (14).
32. Featherstone, *Resistance, Space and Political Identities*, 18.
33. See Carretta, *Equiano, The African*.
34. Cited in Tim Adams, "The Interview: Cultural hallmark," *Observer*, 22 September 2007, accessed 4 March 2014, http://www.theguardian.com/society/2007/sep/23/communities.politicsphilosophyandsociety.
35. The phrase "optimistic imaginary" is used by Shelia Rowbotham in the introduction to her book, *Dreamers of a New Day: Women Who Invented the Twentieth Century* (London: Verso, 2010).
36. Catherine Impey, "Some Diverse Views of Social Equality," *Village Album* 38, c. 1885. Alfred Gillett Trust, Street, Somerset.
37. Catherine Impey to Albion Tourgée, March 1893, The *Albion W. Tourgée* Papers 6772, Chautauqua County Historical Society, Westfield, New York.
38. Catherine Impey, "Some Diverse Views of Social Equality."
39. *Anti-Caste*, December 1892, 2.
40. I have written more extensively about Catherine Impey's and Celestine Edward's work in Caroline Bressey, *Empire, Race and the Politics of Anti-Caste* (London: Bloomsbury Academic, 2013).
41. Ibid.
42. *Anti-Caste*, December 1889, 2–3.
43. Ibid., 2–3.
44. "Outline Sketch of the Life of S J Celestine Edwards," *Fraternity*, May 1895, 3–4.
45. For examples of the kind of talks Edwards gave see the *Hampshire Advertiser*, 3 September 1887, 2.
46. *Portsmouth Evening News*, 14 August 1893, 2.
47. *Fraternity*, April 1894, 12.
48. *Fraternity*, November 1893, 12.

49. Bressey, *Empire, Race and the Politics of Anti-Caste.*
50. See Marilyn Lake and Henry Reynolds, *Drawing the Global Colour Line: White Men's Countries and the International Challenge of Racial Equality* (Cambridge: Cambridge University Press, 2008).
51. Jonathan Hyslop, "The Imperial Working Class Makes Itself 'White': White Labourism in Britain, Australia, and South Africa before the First World War," *Journal of Historical Sociology* 12, no. 4 (1999): 398–421.
52. For a discussion of early critics of *The Making,* see F. K. Donnelly, "Ideology and Early English Working Class History: Edward Thompson and His Critics," *Social History* 1, no. 2 (1976): 219–238.
53. See Bressey, *Empire, Race and the Politics of Anti-Caste.*
54. Ibid.

Chapter 6

E. P. Thompson and the Kitchen Sink or Feeling from Below, c. 1963

Lara Kriegel

Introduction: Making and Losing

If the final pronouncement of E. P. Thompson's *The Making of the English Working Class* had escaped us, we have come, in assessing and commemorating it at the half-century mark, to know the concluding gambit very well. As he closed his magisterial tome, Thompson lamented that "something [had been] lost." "We cannot be sure how much," he noted, for "we are among the losers."[1] Taken in its most immediate context, these words express regret about the lost potential of radicalism and romanticism to combine as critical forces in a battle against utilitarianism. The failure, Thomson indicated, was made manifest with the passage of the Great Reform Act of 1832, which, among other things, foreclosed the possibilities of universal manhood suffrage, at least for the nineteenth century.

Although Thompson concluded his account with these nineteenth-century disappointments, his *Making of the English Working Class* is a meditation on loss more generally, functioning on a number of levels that have to do with narrative, retrospection, and reading. Loss, I would argue, is central to Thompson's narrative. On a manifest level *The Making of the English Working Class* is concerned to articulate, of course, how "class happens." It "happens," Thompson explained, when "men, as a result of common experiences (inherited or shared), feel and articulate the identity of their interests as between themselves, and as against other men whose interests are different from (and usually opposed to) theirs."[2] This process, according to Thompson, was the means through which class consciousness developed. In the case of the English working class, the experience of loss was central to that making or happening. To this end, Pamela Fox has noted in her excellent study of proletarian fiction that "working-class culture carries with it a tradition of lack or loss, as well as revolt."[3] Several references to "loss" appear throughout *The Making*. By and large, deployments of the term come in reference to what are, on the surface, material matters, whether the "loss of status" or the "loss of time" experienced by the artisanal orders. But these developments carry social, and perhaps affective, significance, as the associated losses of "commons" and "community," and "pride" and "independence," so well indicate.[4] In *The Making*, moreover, Thompson gave the sense that these nineteenth-century losses, material and affective in their nature, reverberated into the time of his text's publication. The book is bounded by considerations of the moment and the legacies of loss. It does, certainly, echo the very sentiments expressed by a title published nearly simultaneously, Peter Laslett's *The World We Have Lost*.[5] At the outset, Thompson expressed the wish that "causes that were lost in England might yet be won in Asia and Africa."[6] In so doing, he prepared readers for his tale of making and losing, which closes, of course, with the declaration that "we are among the losers." These words haunt us every time we revisit *The Making*. Perhaps Thompson's tome might just as aptly be titled, to borrow from another magnum opus in British history, *The Decline and Fall of the British Proletariat*.[7]

Speculation about titles notwithstanding, there is something about loss that seems central to the story of the working class as lived, written, and read. It seems to be a matter that implicates the past and the present, and one that involves the material and the social. Class, as Annette Kuhn has noted, is a matter that exists "beneath your clothes, under your skin, in your psyche, at the very core of your being."[8] Aided by this understanding, perhaps we might consider loss, as rendered by Thompson, as the affect of the working class. If affect straddles emotion and reason, and body and mind, it is as capacious a category as class.[9] There is something at once palpable and ineffable about loss as a phenomenon. It might give way to nostalgia. It can also find its expression as emotion. It seems, in the case of working class experience, that it finds its expression in envy and anger. While the attention of historians has turned lately to the consideration of emotion and affect, the history of feeling from below has yet to be written.[10] This is the case despite the fact that historians and literary critics working with emotion have noted its bases in the realm of the social. Yet an excavation of feeling from below is a worthy project, for a host of reasons. A consideration of emotion allows us to get at the experience of collective loss wrought by class formation and its reverberations across centuries. An undertaking of this sort follows upon the aspirations of Thompson's own work. At the same time, this endeavor allows us to reposition Thompson's story, placing it, as I do here, alongside some of the influential cultural productions of his own moment. Finally, it seems that an enterprise of this sort has the unintended effect of enabling us to revisit critiques of Thompson and to address some of the limitations of his considerations of class.

As the musings on loss that bookend Thompson's magisterial tome suggest, *The Making* is not only a history of the eighteenth- and nineteenth-century past. It is also a meditation on Thompson's own present. It is no secret that Thompson was deeply engaged with the politics of his own moment and with the lives of working people. He and his contemporaries learned from students, unionists, and wool packers. Cognizant of the situated nature of his writing, those who have offered critical perspectives on Thompson have placed him within the contexts of university trends, labor politics, and leftist thought. They have located him not only in the national context of England, but also in the international contexts of Cold War Europe and the postcolonial world.[11] But scholarship has been slower to place Thompson within a broader cultural zeitgeist.

The year that saw the publication of *The Making*, 1963, was a heady one for cultural production and political culture in Great Britain. The Profumo Scandal shocked a nation and took the Conservative Party out of office. The Beatles sparked the golden age of Rock and Roll, as they became an international phenomenon. And a number of "kitchen sink" dramas, which were part of the broader phenomenon of the British New Wave, debuted in cinemas.[12] These included *A Place to Go, The Sporting Life,* and *Billy Liar.* Derived oftentimes from plays and novels, these productions drew upon a kitchen sink aesthetic that sought to portray the grim and gritty realm of everyday working class life in such locations as the East End of London, Midlands factory towns, and Lancashire cities through the prism of realism. In content, tone, and setting, these works marked a substantial shift from the upper class parlor dramas long popular on stage and screen. As their own staging grounds, they often took the claustrophobic confines of the working class dwelling and the industrial city street. Such bleak environs suggested the limitations of individual possibility, the monotony of a social landscape and, with them, the confines of a precarious world. In these stark locales, outbursts of anger and expressions of envy punctuate monotonous routine as the intimate practices of everyday life rub up against the class politics of the moment.[13]

It is to this archive that I wish to turn to get at the "structure of feeling" that characterized working class life at the moment when Thompson wrote and published *The Making*.[14] I focus on three examples from this archive. The first is John Osborne's *Look Back in Anger,* which was first performed as a play in London in 1956 and soon after adapted for the screen in 1959. Iconoclastic in its content and daring in its story, this title is considered to be the first of the kitchen sink dramas. The second is *A Kind of Loving,* published as a novel by Stan Barstow in 1960 and made into a film in 1962. With its bleak industrial cityscapes and small pleasures that recall L. S. Lowry's paintings, *A Kind of Loving* shows, quite aptly, the ways in which loss of opportunity and loss of autonomy give rise to feelings of anger and envy. The third, which I address by way of conclusion, is *A Taste of Honey,* Shelagh Delany's work presented as a play on London's fringe in 1958 and adapted for cinema in 1961. Written when the author was a mere eighteen years old, it takes the challenging subject matter of kitchen sink realism to a new level as it explores the question of sexuality and the afterlife of empire.

Along with the genre more generally, these texts share a number of elements. They are works with bleak settings and limited horizons; they involve generational clashes and triangulations; and they include pregnancies (and, in two cases, miscarriages) and domestic resolutions (of varying sorts).[15] Taken together, these assessments of lived experience on a small scale provide a contrast to Thompson's grand epic narrative. As such, they allow for a focus on the emotive responses to the grand story of making and unmaking that Thompson sketched. In considering these texts, we are reminded not only of Thompson's prescience, but also of his myopia, particularly when it came to considerations of gendered experience and global formation.

Part I: Anger and Anomie

Let us begin in the year 1956, an anxious and transformative one on many scores—the Suez Crisis rocked British politics, Fidel Castro landed in Cuba, and the Russians invaded Hungary. This last event upset E. P. Thompson so much, he decided in that year to leave the Communist Party. As these events were unfolding, John Osborne's play, *Look Back in Anger,* premiered at the Royal Court Theater. In the play, Osborne explored a family drama that unraveled in the context of the moment. The time of the play, not incidentally, is denoted in the script as "the present."[16] As if to disavow Conservative prime minister Harold MacMillan's nearly simultaneous pronouncement that "most of our people have never had it so good," the protagonist, Jimmy Porter, announces that "the present" is a moment of foreclosure, gloom, and limitation. "It's pretty dreary living in the American age—unless you're an American, of course," Jimmy declares.[17]

In his capacity as Osborne's alter ego, Jimmy expresses the limitations felt by a class and a generation in this American age. Jimmy appears, essentially, as bored, stuck, and angry. This is, at least in part, an effect of the mismatch between his occupation as a sweet stall owner, which is perhaps meant to be ironic, given Jimmy's bitter outlook and trenchant wit, and his education, which has not delivered on its promises. Whereas Osborne had no tertiary education to speak of, Jimmy had attended a redbrick university; that is, one founded in the nineteenth century in the industrial heart of England to educate the new bourgeoisie. Yet Jimmy remains steadfastly identified with the working class and its long history. This identification is expressed most clearly by Cliff, Jimmy's friend and coworker, who explains that Jimmy understands himself as "common," perhaps even "common as dirt." "We both come from working people," he notes. Some of Jimmy's mother's relatives are "posh," but he identifies far more with his father, whose life story embodied a sad history of the British Left. As Jimmy tells it, his father was a "feverish failure of a man," one who had gone to fight the war in Spain and came home to die. Hopelessness and the anger that come from this experience of finding oneself on the wrong side of history are Jimmy's birthrights. Friends generously assay that Jimmy was "born too late"—that he belonged, more properly in the French Revolution or among the Victorians. But Jimmy, a reader of the *New Statesman,* explains his temperament more bluntly, as he declares, "You see, I learnt at an early age what it was to be angry—angry and helpless."[18]

Although the history he crafts is far more heroic, Thompson gestures to the anger of the working classes in *The Making.* It is, in his formulation, part and parcel of the radicalization of the artisanal classes, for whom "ideal and real grievances" having to do with the loss of pride, hope, and opportunity "combined to shape their anger."[19] As the title of Osborne's play indicates, anger arises when the legacies of the past, the realities of the present, and the forecast for the future collide. Osborne's alter ego, Jimmy, inhabits a dreary present of monotony and anomie, as his Sunday musings at the finish of a long weekend so well indicate. Along with his friend Cliff, he has wasted away the day "reading the papers, drinking tea," while his wife has done the ironing at the board that occupies so prominent a place in the stage set. "Nobody thinks, nobody cares. No beliefs, no convictions, and no enthusiasm. Just another Sunday evening," he laments. But his anomie gives way to anger, as expressed in his speech, and even more so in his very affect. The stage directions urge the performance of a Jimmy whose "anger cools and hardens," whose "voice crumples in disabled rage," and whose laughter is even angry, as it sardonically "roars."[20]

Angry in word and affect, Jimmy is at war with the past, as it is embodied in the parents of his unlikely wife, Alison. Alison's father, Colonel Redfern, holds fast to the patriotism of Queen, God, and Country. Having left England in 1914 not to return until 1947, he inhabits a temporal bubble as he moves through his later years. If there is any doubt as to how Redfern should be played, Osborne leaves the notes that this career soldier is "slightly withdrawn and uneasy," for he lives now "in a world where his authority has become lately less and less unquestionable." As his daughter

Alison sees it, her "poor old daddy" is "just one of those sturdy old plants left over from the Edwardian Wilderness that can't understand why the sun isn't shining anymore." Redfern's own nostalgic retrospection reminds us of the ways in which class structure and imperial formation combine on an affective level. The reverberations of this combination resound well into the post-imperial age, when old army officers waxed nostalgic for a place, a time, and an order that stood at various distances. "I had the Maharajah's army to command—that was my world and I loved it, all of it," Redfern recalls. "If only it could have gone on forever." Redfern's nostalgic patriotism is at odds with Jimmy's anger, as the latter well notes, while signaling, too, the global coordinates of class formation and its affects. "People like me aren't supposed to be patriotic," alleges Jimmy, as he portrays himself as a disaffected cosmopolitan. "We get our cooking from Paris, our politics from Moscow, and our morals from Port Said."[21]

There is, without question, a large dose of misogyny in Jimmy's rage, which is further uncorked by the notion that the age of chivalry, and with it, of the "old white charger," is irrevocably gone. Jimmy's words certainly suggest as much. Of Alison's mother, he quips, "the old bitch should be dead." Elsewhere, he refers to her as a "noble female rhino." Jimmy's antipathies extend to the "royalty" of "middle-class womanhood" more generally. His poor wife Alison bears the brunt of the rage. Time and again, he heckles her, calling her "pusillanimous" and taunting her with that term. Stage directions instruct Jimmy's character to shout, throw, and snatch. He has, it appears, a sadistic desire to see Alison in pain and discomfort, largely, though not only, on an emotional level. There is wisdom combined with Alison's apparent weakness, however, as she explains that Jimmy married not for love, but rather for "revenge." Alison understands well the sources of the disaffectedness among the men around her. "You're hurt because everything's changed. Jimmy's hurt because everything's the same," she tells her father. "And neither of you can face it. Something's gone wrong somewhere, hasn't it?"[22]

These miseries play out on the stage set, a dreary, one-room Midlands flat, whose environs are strewn with newspapers, crowded by an ironing board, and leavened by stuffed animals. Jimmy's friend Cliff describes the room as "a battlefield," and, even more strikingly, as "a very narrow strip of hell." As he seeks to protect Allison, he tells her that Jimmy "hates all of us." Unable to withstand the ire, Allison escapes to her parents' house, only to return to Jimmy after a miscarriage. There is, ultimately, no escape for the pair but into childish and sentimental domestic bliss, as the play ends with the two engaging in a silly couples' game. It seems, at least for the moment, to enable a truce as it keeps Jimmy's anger at bay.[23]

The notion of the "Angry Young Man" might have been something of a media invention.[24] That said, this invention found powerful form on stage and screen in John Osborne's Jimmy Porter, a figure who captured the attention of the nation. As he rendered the character of Jimmy Porter,

Osborne gave shape to the anger of a class and a generation. There was, as the play's life and afterlife suggests, great power in this rendering. But it did have its limits as well, particularly when it came to political action. As William Reddy has noted, emotion carried great force in political discourse, particularly in the eighteenth century and in the romantic era.[25] Afterward, I contend, it did continue to mobilize social movements. Here and there, in fact, Thompson gestured to its force in so doing. The power of Osborne's portrait, however, appears ripe, yet limiting. Anger may be Jimmy Porter's inheritance, but it is not an inspiration for action. Instead, it is a response to longing and to loss, and one that seems to dissipate in the face of domesticity's saccharine sentimentality.

Part II: Love and Envy

While Jimmy Porter punishes women, he is himself feminized at the end of Osborne's play.[26] With this feminization, we might assume, comes the foreclosure not just of anger, but also of a critical political potential. Taken together, Osborne's plotting and the resultant understanding belie a larger concern in radical culture about the tendencies of women and the social processes in which they engage—notably, domesticity and consumption—to foreclose the radical possibilities of class politics. Where the understandings of historical subjects stopped and those of historians began on this score, it is difficult to say. As a host of feminist critics have noted, Thompson's story of class "happening" was unabashedly male.[27] Similarly, the notion of the "culture of consolation" that developed around formations such as the music hall, as explained by Stedman Jones and others, discards the value of that which is popular and consumable—and, ultimately, that which is associated with women. This is an understanding that cultural critics such as F. R. Leavis, who suggested that popular leisure activities made for a passive society, anticipated, too.[28]

These understandings provide one context in which we might understand another of the kitchen sink dramas of the British New Wave: *A Kind of Loving*. This 1962 film took as its inspiration a novel of the same name published two years before and shares a good deal with *Look Back in Anger* in both its landscape and its plot devices. And, like *Look Back in Anger*, it concludes with a sense of domesticity restored, albeit as a consolation of sorts.

It is worthwhile to look more closely for a moment at the film for, while *Look Back in Anger* used a realist aesthetic for the purposes of trenchant critique, *A Kind of Loving* looks to realism to represent the everyday lives of the working classes in the later 1950s and early 1960s on the big screen. Here, we enter the places of work, leisure, and rest that the working classes of Lancashire frequented. We glimpse their small pleasures—be they white weddings or window shopping, brass band concerts or ballrooms, sex or cinema. The film takes us into the close living spaces of the working classes, the crowded kitchen tables, and the claustrophobic living rooms, as it suggests the narrow horizons of the protagonists' lives. It exposes us to the cadences of their chatty speech in thick northern accents that verge upon dialect. All of this transpires against the backdrop of a bleak industrial landscape reminiscent of an L. S. Lowry painting. As if to offer an endpoint to Thompson's story, *A Kind of Loving* was filmed on location in Manchester, Salford, and Bolton, all of which also feature in *The Making*.

If the setting aspires to be true to life, so too do the portrayals of the leading couple, which draw on stereotype rather than breaking the mold, as was the case in *Look Back in Anger. A Kind of Loving* spins the overdetermined tale of a young draughtsman, Vic, and a gamine typist, Ingrid, who work together at a factory. During their courtship, the couple flirt on busses, walk through arcades, and rendezvous in secret. As it all transpires, an increasingly chatty Ingrid asks a mild-mannered Vic, "you don't think I'm common, do you?" It appears that Vic does, but he "goes around" with her, all the same. Their love affair leads, predictably, to an unanticipated pregnancy and, afterward, to an undesired marriage, at least for Vic. The cascading effects of the foreclosure of opportunity wrought by the pregnancy lead the once easygoing Vic to become increasingly angry. It is not only the loss of upward mobility for this young man, the son of an engine driver, that prompts despair, it is also the unsettling travails wrought by Ingrid's petty and meddling mother. The couple resides with her in an exceedingly claustrophobic domestic arrangement, the frustrations of which drive Vic to drink. When he arrives home after a pub-crawl, Ingrid's mother repudiates him with the fiercely uttered, and perfectly placed, chide: "You filthy pig; you filthy disgusting pig." Nevertheless, these hostilities dissipate, at least for a time. As in *Look Back in Anger*, similar plot elements allow for a conclusion of calm consolation. A miscarriage works to quell domestic uncertainty. Additionally, the couple escapes from the older generation, settling, in all senses of the term, into a humble living situation on their own.

A Kind of Loving may share plot elements with *Look Back in Anger*. It differs, however, in the kind of realism to which it aspires—melodramatic in its narrative pulsations, but nonetheless diagnostic in its social types. As we have seen, Vic is, inevitably, spurred to anger. He is driven to this point, we are led to think, in no small part by the nature of the feminine desire that surrounds him—whether for things, for comforts, or for escapes. In a time-honored tradition, Ingrid's appetite for coats, an appetite that is indulged by her mother, proves especially enervating. The garish wallpaper and terrycloth robes that fill the maternal home seem to signal comfort, however, the dreary existence they suggest prompts nothing but unease in Vic—and in the viewers of the film. In addition, Ingrid's mother, a woman characterized by bitterness and dissatisfaction, blames Vic for denying her the pleasures of a white wedding, the destination toward which so many of the era both plotted and pined, as Clare Langhamer has recently shown.[29] Time and again, Vivian, and her mother even more so, articulate these longings in ceaseless chatter that circulates above the incessant din of the television (Ingrid is, of course, named after the film star). But, as her speech so well shows, Ingrid's mother does not simply desire, she also despises. As she jealously guards the security offered by her terraced house, Ingrid's mother lashes out against labor, and unionized labor in particular. In her understanding, busmen, miners, and railway men—that is, the stock from which Victor hails—combine to push up the cost of living. The injustice of it all is particularly sharp, it seems to her, in a world where miners earn £40 per week, while a retired colonel must work at a car park to get by. Like the empire that the colonel must have served, it is all a disappointment. "You can't rely on anybody these days; they promise to deliver and then they let you down," the matriarch declares.

Those familiar with Carolyn Steedman's *Landscape for a Good Woman* might here recall the maternal figure rendered in its pages. Certainly, in Ingrid's mother, we find a cinematic representation of the working class envy and conservatism that fueled Steedman's own mother.[30] Published in 1987, her portrait was both vivid and prescient of recent scholarly trends. In her landmark work *Ugly Feelings,* Sianne Ngai revealed the political valences and timeliness of such states as irritation, paranoia, and, of course, envy, for our moment.[31] Frances Ferguson has endeavored to offer a literary history of envy, one that is tied up in the rise of democratic institutions such as the school.[32] Well before Steedman, Ngai, and Ferguson had left their mark, left-leaning cultural critics of the twentieth century tended to see the structures of envy that seemed to arise out of female desire as dangerous for, or distracting from, the formation of a radical class consciousness. Acquisitiveness, they suggested, is necessarily atomizing, while domesticity is, by nature, distracting. As they have sought to recover feminine desire of all sorts, feminist critics have endeavored to recuperate envy in the name of collective politics.[33]

At first glance, it appears that there is little that is redemptive in the envy expressed by Ingrid and, even more so, by her mother. Oddly, however, the very project of portraying envy in *A Kind of Loving* may have feminist repercussions, for it partakes of the very strategies that feminist historians have employed to query and shatter Thompson's masculine narrative. If Thompson portrayed class on an epic scale, feminist historians have looked to the small space of the household to capture the lived experiences of women and the gendered valences of class. In *The Struggle for the Breeches,* Anna Clark brought gender into the story of class formation by focusing on the social arrangements of domesticity and the cultural valences of melodrama. In "The Tale of Samuel and Jemima," Catherine Hall illuminated the difference that gender makes in class formation and radical politics as she honed in on the divergent experiences of a domestic pair as they lived through 1819's Peterloo Massacre.[34] Similarly, *A Kind of Loving* explores the diminishing possibilities for a young couple as they play out against the gritty backdrop of industrial Lancashire. Read alongside this body of scholarship, the film brings the gendered contours of working class existence into view. Read alongside *The Making*, it allows us to see, once again, the centrality of loss, in its manifold forms, to a long history of working class existence. Perhaps this set piece of New-Wave film has more critical potential than we might have thought.

Part III: Tasting and Transcending

Performed in London's fringe in 1958 and made into a film three years later, Shelagh Delany's *A Taste of Honey* pushes the vistas and the critical potential of kitchen sink drama to new levels. Like our preceding objects of analysis, *A Taste of Honey* portrays a grim and limited working class existence, in this instance in Salford, near Manchester. Like *Look Back in Anger*, the play's action transpires, primarily, in a "comfortless flat," one that is cold and stark, lacking both heat and lampshades. Directed by Tony Richardson, the film adaptation takes its viewers beyond the flat, through sites of working class consumption and entertainment, among them, a shoe shop, an amusement park, and the iconic Blackpool promenade, not unlike *A Kind of Loving*.[35] In the process, like *A Kind of Loving*, it spotlights desire, or want, yet it does so on the broadest of scales. Jo, the protagonist, who is on the cusp of eighteen, longs not only for an engagement ring, but also for an education; she wishes not simply for clothes, but for companionship as well; and while she wants for money, she desires, more than anything else, to have a mother.

This extended wish list suggests that Jo is, in many regards, a different protagonist than those considered above and that *A Taste of Honey* is, in many respects, a different sort of production. Certainly, it involves the essential ingredients of cramped quarters, triangulated relationships, and unwanted pregnancy. But gone is any pretense of respectability through socialization by an older generation. In keeping with the spirit of the customary festivals spotlighted in the play and the film, including Guy Fawkes' Day, the world evoked here is a world turned upside down, one where youth both rule and raise adults. Gone, too, is the security of wedlock, even of the sort where one muddles through. The play's sensibilities do not admit of marriage as a viable institution. Jokingly, Jo and her boyfriend engage in a banter that refers to entrapment in a "barbaric cult"—not "Mau Mau," which would have carried purchase with the original audience, but rather "marriage."[36] More than the stuff of witty repartee, marriage—or, more properly, its impossibility—is central to the plot. In fact, it is explicitly denied on three occasions. We learn at the outset that Jo is fatherless; her mother Helen is a drunken "semi-whore." Time and again, Helen is unlucky in love. The commencement of the play finds Helen whisked off by Peter, a hard drinking and hard talking veteran, who tires of her in the end. And Jo, who seeks comfort in teenage courtship, finds herself by the play's end at the verge of giving birth, with the father, Jimmie, nowhere to be found. "He came in with Christmas and went out with the New Year," Jo recounts to a friend.[37]

A Taste of Honey challenges the limits of the genre of the kitchen sink drama in more ways than this, however. There is, most notably, the fact that Jo's pregnancy is the result of an interracial affair. Jimmie, it turns out, is a black British seaman enlisted in the Navy. This is a matter that Delany exploits to great effect as she offers up exchanges that challenge the wit and sensibilities of the audience. Jimmie and Jo imagine a romance where he is Othello and she, Desdemona. When Jo, convinced that her lover has "a little bit of jungle" in him, asks Jimmie whether he hails from Africa, he offers a deadpan reply: "Cardiff. Disappointed?" This does not stop Jo, later on, from imagining Jimmy, by that moment departed, as an African prince. Additionally, upon learning that her daughter is to give birth to a black child, Helen inquires, in her panicked surprise, "What about the nurse? She's going to get a bit of a shock, isn't she?" To this query, Jo bluntly replies, "She's black, too."[38] While the Shakespeare banter offers a display of cleverness, these latter two moments show a deep and sharp understanding of the racialized politics of labor in Great Britain, particularly in the postwar era. Jimmie may hail from Cardiff, but he is clearly tied in his history to the African enslaved population that was, at once, an international proletariat in its own right, as well as an unacknowledged engine in the making of the English working class. We meet Jimmie at the moment when members of that proletariat were migrating to Great Britain to serve the growing apparatuses of the newly nationalized transportation services and the recently instituted National Health Service. Fittingly, perhaps, Jimmie was a nurse before devoting himself to the Navy. As such, he exhibits a nurturing capacity that, once again, punctures the scripts of the kitchen sink drama, with him offering care to Jo, if only fleetingly, when she is hungry or hurt.

A Taste of Honey challenges the understood limits of national history, gender roles, and class formation, but it does not stop there. It also provides, at least temporarily, an alternative to the unhappy domestic life of the normative working class family, which serves to breed envy and anger. The second act of the play finds Jo having taken up house, quite happily, with her friend Geoff, who is an art student and a character derided by Helen as a "pansified little freak." Geoff plays "nursemaid" to Jo, as he helps her confront her fears. Together, the two strive to create a home that provides a welcome respite from the unhappy interiors we have seen in other instances of kitchen sink realism, not to mention in the first act of *A Taste of Honey* itself. They flirt with amorous behaviors and play at heterosexual marriage, albeit with a degree of gender reversal, wherein Geoff cooks, cleans, and cares for the pregnant Jo. There is space here for the banter of working class couples. There is room, too, on Jo's part, at least in the film version, for some prurient curiosity about homosexual acts, which were not decriminalized in Britain until 1967. She inquires of Geoff, plaintively,

"I want to know what you do. I want to know why you do it." Amidst it all, the couple settles into what appears to be a happy domesticity and even a veritable love affair. "I'd sooner be dead than away from you," Geoff tells the pregnant Jo. With a hint of premonition, she replies, mournfully, "We can't be like this forever."[39]

In her perceptive assessment of *A Taste of Honey*, Terry Lovell noted that Jo faced a choice between the "sexuality" offered by Jimmy and the "domesticity" held out by Geoff.[40] She could not have both. In the end, she has neither. As the production draws to a close, it is Jo's wayward mother Helen—returned from her failed marriage to the intemperate Peter—who punctures the cozy, if short-lived, home life that Geoff and Jo had created. "And what's your part in this little Victorian melodrama? Nursemaid?" Helen asks, as she taunts Geoff, eventually driving him away in opposition to her daughter's desires.[41] The story's end thus finds the unsteady mother-daughter pair awaiting the arrival of Jo's mixed race child.

If it destroys any hope of masculine protection, whether on the part of Jimmy, Geoff, or Peter, *A Taste of Honey*'s conclusion does not offer up an image of a rosy cross-generational matriarchy. Granted, it does not resort to the narrative device of miscarriage—an ultimate, albeit unexamined loss for a pregnant woman—in the ways that *Look Back in Anger* and *A Kind of Loving* do.[42] Neither does it offer a happy resolution in birth. Instead, the narrative, which follows the gestational cycle nearly to its end, unleashes a stream of ambivalences about motherhood—and especially, though not exclusively, working class motherhood. As he tried to help Jo come to terms with her pregnancy, Geoff had suggested, at one point, "You can get rid of babies before they're born, you know." This is an utterance of no small consequence at a moment when abortion remained illegal in Britain and before the pill was introduced in December 1961. On another occasion, he remonstrated a recalcitrant Jo: "Motherhood is supposed to come natural to woman." But Jo remains skeptical and resistant. "I hate motherhood," she declares.[43] And though her own mother returns to make tea and reminisce, she offers no evidence that Jo should feel otherwise.

Ultimately, then, *A Taste of Honey* substantiates and extends the sense of loss that E. P. Thompson sought to articulate in *The Making*. The film, particularly, nods toward a sense of an organic working class community whose passing was mourned by Thompson, as it showcases traditional children's songs, Empire Day parades, and Guy Fawkes bonfires. It shows this community to be fleeting, existing in snippets and memories only. In so doing, it makes us all witnesses to that loss.[44] Yet *A Taste of Honey* operates on another level, too, as it spins the story of Jimmy, Geoff, Helen, and especially Jo. Jo is an outsider among the dispossessed, for whom the community of a fading world and the compensations of consumer culture, with its cheap Woolworth rings and its frilly baby cots, can offer little comfort. Nor can heterosexual domesticity or maternal companionship hold out security. Instead, Jo's plight is to live with loss on top of loss.

Conclusion: Anger and After

It is all too easy to look back at kitchen sink realism with a degree of nostalgia. Certainly, nostalgia fuelled the affective economies of many of the characters that appeared in the works discussed here. It is a governing affect of the kitchen sink genre, as the very title *Look Back in* Anger suggests. And today, it is through a nostalgic rendering that many of us connect to the very genre. I am thinking, of course of the 1996 hit by the Manchester-based band Oasis, "Don't Look Back in Anger." The song refers not only to the seminal work of the Angry Young Men, but also to innumerable Beatles' tunes. The effect, ultimately, is a gesture to a past that is no anger, and all nostalgia. If the Oasis hit is any indication, perhaps nostalgia is the after-effect of loss, once the anger and envy are emptied out.

There is a great deal of nostalgia for the English working class these days, at a moment when its earlier form is all but lost, and at a time when the accouterments of a proletarian class have become the stuff of fashion. Whether aesthetic or economic in nature, nostalgic practices extend across the cultural spectrum. Take, for instance, the L. S. Lowry retrospective that debuted in July 2013 at the Tate Britain, a museum built, not incidentally, through profits acquired by means of enslaved and indentured labor. It was the first metropolitan retrospective for the Lancashire-born artist (1887–1976), whose paintings, many completed during the heyday of the British New Wave, appear as if they might offer a stage set for *A Kind of Loving*. Lowry is something of an enigma, as he was not a man who fussed a great deal over his aesthetic process. "You don't need brains to be a painter," he once maintained, "just feelings."[45] As it featured the man and his work, the show stoked nostalgia for the English working class at a moment of its disappearance. This fact was not lost on the exhibit's curators and designers, who made it explicitly clear in the exhibition's texts and publicity.

Less examined, though at least as fascinating, was the marketing of nostalgia in the museum's gift shop. Upon exiting the show, exhibition-goers encountered an elegantly displayed array of bowler hats and neckties. This display sought literally to capitalize upon the working class chic that is au courant in a London where modern British cuisine is all the rage and where East End property prices are through the roof. These garments tapped into a pervasive nostalgia; so too did the impressive display of books at the exhibit's shop. Placed front and center for visiting tourists and art lovers to purchase were an impressive array of titles. Foremost among them was, of course, *The Making of the English Working Class*.

What are we to make of the appearance of E. P. Thompson's tome in the gift shop at the Tate Britain? It may be that class consciousness has found its way to the museum. It is more likely, however, that *The Making of the Working Class* has joined the paintings of L. S. Lowry and the artifacts of kitchen sink drama as memorials to a world that is no more. If *The Making of the Working Class* sought to capture the losses of the industrial proletariat, it had a lasting impact, too, as a monument to its own time, providing a deep background to and an affective touchstone for the social politics and class feelings of its moment of publication. Its dual concerns with a political crossroads in the nineteenth century and with its own time of writing resonate with one another. And they continue to reach us today. They may appear to be devoid of their power, commoditized and aestheticized in the gift shop at the Tate Britain. Speaking less cynically, however, we should note that the text endures, newly available for expanding audiences. This may not have been the dénouement that E. P. Thompson anticipated. Yet all, it seems, is not lost.

***Lara Kriegel** is Associate Professor of History and English at Indiana University, Bloomington. A social and cultural historian, she has focused her work on the ways that materialized experience and meaning making have intersected in the modern British world. In recent years, she has tracked the ways that Victorian warfare shaped both national institutions and ordinary lives across a longue duree from the nineteenth through the twenty-first-century. Her book,* The Crimean War and its Afterlife: Making Modern Britain, *is forthcoming with Cambridge University Press.*

Notes

I wish to thank Antoinette Burton and Stephanie Seawell for their work and care in organizing the conference at which the paper was presented that occasioned this article.

1. E. P. Thompson, *The Making of the English Working Class* (New York: Vintage Books, 1966), 830.
2. Ibid., 9.
3. Pamela Fox, *Class Fictions: Shame and Resistance in the British Working Class Novel, 1890–1945* (Durham, NC: Duke University Press, 1994), 8.
4. Thompson, *The Making,* 203, 214, 216–217, 262, 264, 273, 276, 280, 310, 408, 416, 445, 447, 706, 759.
5. Peter Laslett, *The World We Have Lost* (London: Menthuen, 1965).
6. Thompson, *The Making,* 13.
7. See David Cannadine, *Decline and Fall of the British Aristocracy* (New York: Vintage Books, 1999).
8. Annette Kuhn, *Family Secrets: Acts of Memory and Imagination* (London: Verso, 1995), 117.
9. See Patricia Tinceneto Clark, ed., *The Affective Turn: Theorizing the Social* (Durham, NC: Duke University Press, 2007); Mary Favret, "The Study of Affect and Romanticism," *Literature Compass* 6, no. 6 (2009): 1159–1166.
10. On the turn to emotion, see Nicole Eustace, Eugenia Lean, Julie Livingston, Jan Plamper, William M. Reddy, and Barbara H. Rosenwein, "*AHR* Conversation: The Historical Study of Emotion," *American Historical Review* 117, no. 5 (2012): 1487–1531.

11. See Joan Allen and Malcolm Chase, "Britain, 1750–1900," in *Histories of Labour: National and International Perspectives*, ed. Joan Allen, Alan Campell, and John McIlroy (Pontypool: Merlin, 2010).
12. Neil Nehring, *Flowers in the Dustbin: Culture, Anarchy and Postwar England* (Ann Arbor: University of Michigan Press, 1993), 235; David Simonelli, *Working Class Heroes: Rock Music and British Society in the 1960s and 1970s* (Lanham, MD: Lexington Books, 2013).
13. See Reade Dornan, "Kitchen Sink Drama," in *Western Drama through the Ages: A Student Reference Guide*, ed. Kimball King (New York: Greenwood, 2007), 452–453. On class and everyday life, see Carolyn Steedman, *An Everyday Life of the English Working Class* (Cambridge: Cambridge University Press, 2013).
14. See, notably, Raymond Williams, *The Country and the City* (London: Chatto, 1973).
15. On the importance of these elements to the Angry Young Men, and to the larger cultural moment, see Stephen Brooke, "Gender and Working Class Identity in Britain during the 1950s," *Journal of Social History* 34, no. 1 (2001): 773–795. See also Peter J. Kalliney, "Cities of Affluence: Masculinity, Class, and the Angry Young Men," *MFS: Modern Fiction Studies* 47, no. 1 (2001): 92–117; Claire Langhamer, *The English in Love: The Intimate Story of an Emotional Revolution* (Oxford: Oxford University Press, 2013); Stephen C. Shafer, "An Overview of the Working Classes in British Feature Film from the 1960s to the 1980s: From Class Consciousness to Marginalization," *International Labor and Working-Class History*, no. 59 (2001): 3–14.
16. John Osborne, *Look Back in Anger* (New York: Dramatic Publishing, 1959), 3.
17. Ibid., 12.
18. Ibid., 24, 46.
19. Thompson, *The Making*, 262.
20. Osborne, *Look Back in Anger*, 10, 12, 47. See also Nehring, *Flowers in the Dustbin*, 199, 235.
21. Osborne, *Look Back in Anger*, 12, 52, 54–55.
22. Ibid., 15–16, 32, 42, 44, 55.
23. Ibid., 53.
24. Nehring, *Flowers in the Dustbin*, 190.
25. William Reddy, *The Navigation of Feeling: A Framework for the History of Emotions* (Cambridge: Cambridge University Press, 2001).
26. Nehring, *Flowers in the Dustbin*, 201.
27. See, most notably, Anna Clark, *The Struggle for the Breeches* (Berkeley: University of California Press, 1997); Catherine Hall, *White, Male and Middle Class* (London: Routledge, 1992); Joan Wallach Scott, *Gender and the Politics of History* (New York: Columbia University Press, 1988).
28. The classic article here, whose tenets have been both adopted and critiqued, is Gareth Stedman Jones, "Working-Class Culture and Working-Class Politics in London, 1870–1900: Notes on the Remaking of a Working Class," *Journal of Social History* 7, no. 4 (1974): 460–508; Nehring, *Flowers in the Dustbin*, 235.
29. Langhamer, *The English in Love*.
30. Carolyn Steedman, *Landscape for a Good Woman: A Story of Two Lives* (New Brunswick, NJ: Rutgers University Press, 1987).
31. Sianne Ngai, *Ugly Feelings* (Cambridge, MA: Harvard University Press, 2005).
32. Frances Ferguson, "Envy Rising," *English Literary History* 69, no. 4 (2002): 889–905.

33. See Pamela Fox, *Class Fictions*, 30–44; Steph Lawler, "'Getting Out and Getting Away': Women's Narratives of Class Mobility," Feminist Review no. 63 (1999): 3–24.
34. Clark, *The Struggle for the Breeches*; Hall, *White, Male, and Middle Class*.
35. Important criticism of the film includes Christine Geraghty, "Women and 60s British Cinema: The Development of the 'Darling' Girl" and Peter Hutchings, "Beyond the New Wave: Realism in British Cinema, 1959–1963," in *The British Cinema Book*, ed. Robert Murphy (Lodnon: British Film Institute, 2001), 101–108 and 146–152; William L. Horne, "Greatest Pleasures," in *The Cinema of Tony Richardson: Essays and Interviews*, ed. James M. Welsh and John C. Tibbets (Albany: State University of New York Press, 1999), 81–126; and Terry Lovell, "Landscapes and Stories in 1960s British Realism," in *Dissolving Views: Key Writings on British Cinema*, ed. Andrew Higson (London: Cassell, 1996), 157–177.
36. Shelagh Delany, *A Taste of Honey* (New York: Modern Classics, 1959), 25.
37. Ibid., 49.
38. Ibid., 25, 86.
39. Ibid., 59, 61, 67.
40. Lovell, "Landscapes and Stories," 172.
41. Delany, *A Taste of Honey*, 61.
42. Thanks to Linda Mitchell for pressing me here.
43. Delany, *A Taste of Honey*, 49, 51, 56.
44. See, for example, Lovell, "Landscapes and Stories," 169, 175.
45. ArtRepublic, accessed 15 March 2014, http://www.artrepublic.com/biographies/111-ls-lowry.html.

Chapter 7

South African Remains

E. P. Thompson, Biko, and the Limits of The Making of the English Working Class

Isabel Hofmeyr

Any book anniversary is an invitation to rereading. As Patricia Meyer Spacks suggests, returning to books already read, we confront "how we, like the books we reread, have both changed and remained the same." Rereading helps us "make sense of ourselves."[1]

The fiftieth anniversary of the publication of *The Making of the English Working Class* has precipitated a flurry of such rereading. Academics, museum practitioners, workers' organizations, and journalists debate the legacies of Thompson's magnum opus, asking what remains of British Marxism, social history, and politically engaged academic work.[2]

In South Africa, where Thompson's work has had a decisive influence, especially in the 1970s and 1980s, there have been a number of such rereadings.[3] Quite rightly, these have celebrated Thompson's importance and outlined the conditions that enabled his work to take hold. Yet these studies evince little interest in the limits of Thompson's circulation. To celebrate his reach is important; appreciating the limits of his work is perhaps more so. Like others who have discussed Thompson's influence in South Africa, my academic career spanned part of the period being discussed. Thinking about the limits of Thompson's work may help curb the strong tendency toward nostalgia that such exercises invariably invite.

This article explores the theme of reading and rereading by placing *The Making* alongside Steve Biko's *I Write What I Like* (*IWWIL*). Such placing is quite literal: the article considers different volumes of these texts owned by South African libraries and the marginalia that these have attracted. These miniature histories of the books are contextualized against the mutually shaping reading formations into which the two texts were folded. With regard to *The Making*, these formations were shaped, on the one hand, by the hyper-nationalism of the antiapartheid era, which sought to create a new nation via a new history and, on the other, by the emergence of the Black Consciousness Movement (BCM), of which Biko's writings formed the key manifesto. As Shireen Ally has argued, the BCM displaced white radicals from revolutionary leadership roles, making them retreat into class analysis that came to function as an analytical alternative to race.[4] As a text that presented a radical configuration of nation and class, *The Making* provided a usable past, or at least a usable model for constructing a class-based version of an antiapartheid past.

British Marxism Meets Black Consciousness in South Africa

That *The Making* exercised a powerful influence in South African intellectual life is beyond question. Thompsonian-style social history inspired a "history from below'" movement that in turn fed into art, drama, public history, and workers' and adult education programs.[5] This influence was perhaps most apparent in the late 1970s and 1980s and is generally ascribed to a steady stream of white South African English academics exposed to British Marxism in the UK, as well as the spectacular reemergence of political and trade union resistance to the apartheid state in the 1970s after the crackdown of the 1960s.[6] These factors helped precipitate a major shift in the social science traditions of white English universities. Previously dominated by a liberal model in which race was seen as an irrational phenomenon that hobbled capitalist development in South Africa, these traditions shifted to a model in which race was understood as intrinsic to the functioning of capitalism. In this analysis of "racial capitalism" class became the key calling card. As different versions of British and continental Marxism circulated in South Africa, exactly what class meant was of course vociferously debated, but these disagreements only served to underline the centrality of Marxist aligned analyses. Such analyses of class however seldom manifested any transnational dimensions given the hyper-nationalism that the antiapartheid struggle generated.

As Shireen Ally has demonstrated, a decisive factor in these developments was the emergence of Black Consciousness (BC).[7] Breaking in 1968 with the National Union of South African Students (in theory a nonracial organization but in fact white-led), a group of black student leaders including Steve Biko established the South African Students Organization (SASO) and began experimenting with ideas and practices that would subsequently be grouped together under the label of BC. Working in church and community groups, debating societies, arts organizations, theological seminaries, and black homeland universities established by the apartheid state, BC activists propagated ideas of psychological liberation and existential freedom that urged black people to use their minds to free themselves from racialized subjugation. As Dan Magaziner argues, the BCM in its early phases established a "political philosophy that called for neither liberation nor power but consciousness."[8] Rooted in an antipolitics that was chary of large-scale movements and their supposed capacities to confer freedom on their followers, BC had a wide reach especially among black intellectuals. In later years there were various attempts to give the movement institutional form, but attacks from both the apartheid state and African National Congress-aligned groups, as well as internecine fights, limited its organizational expression and reach. Historiographically the BCM has been cold-shouldered by the dominance of ANC-aligned interpretations and, apart from its most prominent figure, Steve Biko who was tortured to death in police custody in 1977, it enters mainstream depictions as a footnote, a grouping that kept resistance alive after the crackdown of the 1960s and helped ignite the Soweto 1976 uprising. Despite this historiographical sidelining, the figure and ideas of Biko and the BCM more generally remain influential: the "new Bikoists" for example have returned to BC ideas as a way of seeking radical solutions to the gross inequalities of contemporary South Africa.[9]

As Ally demonstrates, it is critical to take the BCM into account in understanding the growth of radical class-based analyses, of which *The Making* formed a part. Faced with a separatist black-led organization, white radicals found themselves without a leadership or revolutionary role. One response to these changed circumstances was to embrace a class-based analysis and/or a nonracial African National Congress-United Democratic Front position. In the words of one commentator, "Marxism was the new religion and the Freedom Charter holy writ."[10] As one leading figure in this white radical configuration explained, Marxism "offered a new generation of white academics an intellectually coherent alternative to Black Consciousness." Ally argues, "What Marxism's class analysis offered this group of intellectuals was not just a powerful theoretical lens to explain apartheid, but a powerful political tool for white intellectuals to deal more comfortably with questions of race."[11] These two traditions of race and class did not of course run on entirely different tracks and there were to be exchanges that went on between Marxist and BC traditions with the latter, for example taking on more class analysis in the 1980s. Because the class/race dynamic forms a central pivot in South African historiography, these conversations continue into the present.

Placing Biko and Thompson alongside each other offers us an opportunity to understand the trajectories of *The Making* in South Africa but equally to grapple with the limits of its reach.

A Tale of Two Missing Texts

Spread across South African libraries are some fifty copies of the *The Making*. These include all English-language editions of the text.[12] The comprehensiveness of these editions provides one measure of the text's impact in South Africa. The British Library by comparison carries only the UK editions.

However, if one looks more carefully at where the editions of *The Making* are held, the reach of the text appears more curtailed. All the copies of the text are housed in university libraries—there are no copies of *The Making* in the public library system in South Africa. This pattern of acquisition took me by surprise. Interested in all volumes and editions of *The Making*, I visited the Johannesburg Public Library (JPL) fully expecting to find some copies there. As matters turned out, the only Thompson book they had acquired was his science fiction novel *The Skyaos Papers*.[13]

Having failed to find *The Making* at the JPL, I decided to take the opportunity to look at the editions of Biko's *IWWIL*. Compiled a year after Biko's death in 1978 from his journalism, speeches, and interviews, the collection was immediately banned in South Africa for both distribution and possession. Any copies in a public library would hence be post-1994 ones. But, again to my surprise, I found the Biko book absent, but in a rather different way. According to its records, the JPL has six copies in its lending section but these have been stolen or have been taken out and never returned, producing the poignant and telling entry "Biko, Steve. Long Overdue." The Harold Strange Africana Library (a non-lending research section of the JPL) did have a copy but of a rather unexpected kind, namely a photocopy in a homemade board binding. As the librarian explained, the book was in huge demand and copies did not survive long. Texts were heavily "mutilated" with marginalia and readers routinely tore out the pages they liked. Having had several editions read to destruction, the library had substituted the bound photocopy, which has to be replaced regularly. There were four pristine editions of *IWWIL* in the library's stacks but these are never allowed near readers. I was of course keen to see the "mutilated" copies but these had long been dispatched to wherever decommissioned books get sent. The librarian was somewhat uncomprehending of why I'd wanted to see such a copy when the library's duty was plainly to preserve its material.

After my JPL visit, I became interested in whether I could track down a "mutilated" copy of *IWWIL* either in the public library or university library sector. I was able to find copies in the Witwatersrand and Cape Town university systems. The University of Johannesburg copies proved elusive: two of their campus libraries (Auckland Park and Soweto) showed copies available but these turned out not to be on the shelves, while a third campus (Doornfontein) indicated that a copy was housed in Special Collections and hence kept under lock and key. Fully expecting to be able to see at least this copy, I set off, but again was disappointed. The Special Collections librarians searched high and low but could find nothing, returning to tell me in a rather melancholic way, that the book must have been stolen.

I phoned various township libraries and inevitably met the same story—"we did have copies but they have been stolen or are long overdue." I did find one library in Alex with a copy in its holdings. I set off immediately and met the librarian with whom I had spoken and she went off to get me the copy. She was gone for some time. "I can't believe it," she said on her return, "the copy was here only a few days ago but now it's disappeared."

Marking Words

This pattern of library distribution of the two books is echoed by the marginalia that the two texts attract. The copies of both texts that I examined are from libraries rather than privately held copies and are hence "institutionalized" volumes, bound in buckram and imprinted with university crests and accession numbers. *The Making* and *IWWIL* have both been used as undergraduate teaching texts and as such they attract what we might regard as "normal" marginalia—warming up the pen; avoidance of work (daydreaming and doodling); using the text as reliquary for photos and personal items; the aide memoire of underlining, highlighting, asterisking, summarizing, inserting post-it notes; and creating a personalized "index" of pages as a customized retrieval system.[14]

In the case of *The Making*, marginalia took the form of underlining, highlighting, and asterisks in the text itself. No words or phrases were written in the margins. There was however one exception, a volume at the University of Cape Town (UCT) library that belonged originally to Julius Lewin, a scholar of law and what was then called African Government (an early avatar of African Studies). Shortly before his death in 1968, Lewin passed the volume on to David Walsh, an African Studies academic in Cape Town. Lewin's volume contains neat marginalia in the back flyleaf of the volume that draw parallels between eighteenth- and early nineteenth-century England and South Africa.

These notations include "Apartheid 177, 616, 626," all pages that focus on Jacobite episodes followed by arrest, imprisonment, and in some cases a narrow escape from the death penalty. An entry "vanity, 159 and 162" deals with the heavy-handed measures and crackdowns taken against members of the London Corresponding Society (LCS). Another entry reads "Thelwall

185 cf SA." An important "character" in *The Making*, Thelwall was a key orator, poet, strategist, and intellectual of the LCS, charged with—and acquitted of—high treason. Page 185 does not in fact mention Thelwall (it deals with the split between revolutionaries and constitutionalists in the LCS), so how Lewin sees this link is not clear. Yet, the Rivonia Trial (1963–1964) at which the high command of the ANC including Mandela narrowly escaped the death sentence could not have been far from his thinking. Further comments include "Peterloo like Sharpeville? 671–2," "Role of Middle Class," "England beyond London," "Whale of a book," "Half-loaf problem," and "packed with concrete detail."

In the bookshelves of other South African academics, there are no doubt similarly annotated copies of *The Making*. As a bibliographic aside, Lewin's copy was the Victor Gollancz edition of 1963. As *The Making* came into its own in South Africa from the 1970s on, it was the blue-spined Pelican edition of 1968 that most people would have owned. Indeed the depth of involvement that many scholars had with the book both in South Africa and elsewhere emerges from their vivid memories of that blue spine—demotically paperback but somehow monumental at the same time.[15] In South Africa, the blue spine could also stand in for Thompson's broader but somewhat diffuse influence, mediated to a student audience by sections of *The Making*, "Time, Work-Discipline, and Industrial Capitalism" and *The Poverty of Theory*.[16] The spine no doubt also captured the totality of a text that was very seldom read from cover to cover.

Yet whatever marginalia those private copies might contain, the library volumes of *The Making* bear no marginalia, beyond, as I have indicated, the standard highlighting and underlining produced by various undergraduate hands.

The university copies of *IWWIL* by contrast provide evidence of a more engaged relationship with the text. The Biko texts certainly contain the standard evidence of undergraduate toiling through print: in addition to the usual underlining, students stop to look up words like "arrogance" and "acutely" and write these definitions in the margins of the book. Students invent their own bookmarks and retrieval systems through inserting phrases like "Start here to read," "Stop," and by making a personalized index of page numbers.[17]

In addition to these pedagogic markings, the edges of the pages are peppered with annotations. Many of these attempt to summarize or transpose the ideas of *IWWIL* into the students' own terms. In several cases, students gloss passages by drawing on vocabulary no doubt culled from lectures and required in essays: "manufacturing hegemony," "false consciousness," "social capital," "life world," and so on.[18] One also encounters comments that arise from a dialogue with the text outside the classroom. "What do we do when we found [*sic*] consciousness" muses one reader, pointing to a major debate about the tactical and strategic difficulties facing any movement propounding psychological and existential liberation.[19] One reader with an interest in campus politics used the marginalia as an opportunity to link Biko's understanding of student politics to contemporary circumstances.[20]

Readers also apply Biko's insights to contemporary South Africa. Next to a passage on black poverty in South Africa in the 1970s, someone writes "New SA." Alongside a discussion of the "white man's integration ... based on exploitative values ... in which black will compete with black, using each other as rungs up a step ladder leading them to white values," we encounter the comment "Post apthd S. A." Next to a passage "No wonder the African child learns to hate his heritage in his days at school. So negative is the image presented to him that he tends to find solace only in close identification with the white society," a comment at the bottom of the page reads "Coconut Theory" (a post-apartheid term designating black middle class students—"black on the outside but white inside") and in the margin at the side of the page, "We need to rewrite our History." Elsewhere the same reader writes, "Black people still need to be emancipated."[21]

Readers also transpose ideas from one domain of experience into another. An essay on "The Definition of Black Consciousness" provides the following explanation:

1. Being black is not a matter of pigmentation—being black is a reflection of a mental attitude.
2. Merely by describing yourself as black you have started on a road towards emancipation, you have committed yourself to fight against all forces that seek to use your blackness as a stamp that mark you out as a subservient being.

Next to this a reader has drawn a line and written "Blessed be the poor," transposing Biko's discourse into a Christian realm and pointing us towards black theology, a strong theme in Biko's thinking and BC more generally.[22]

Elsewhere, a paragraph on Christian missionaries as agents of imperialism attracted the following: "Wrong"; "makes blacks look stupid"; and "? ? What ? Worship no God But me." The paragraph describes missionaries as extorting conversion through emphasizing the terrors of hell and denigrating existing religious beliefs and cultural values. While this paragraph does not capture the full range of Biko's thought on Christianity in Africa, it does reflect an anticolonial tendency to understand Christian missions through an inverse image of their own account of themselves. While anticolonial accounts condemn Christian mission activity, they do nonetheless attribute considerable power to them. Converts by contrast are seen as having less agency. The recent historiography on Christian evangelism by contrast suggests that Christianity in Africa is in fact spread by Africans who broker the new religious ideas into their communities. The reader's critique points us in this direction.[23]

In another instance of transposition, a reader "translates" Biko into idioms of popular culture. In the white space across the top of the contents page, a reader has scrawled in angled lines:

SASO,
SASO
I ryt
What
I lyk[24]

Here the title of the book appears to be translated into text-speak while the rhythmical insistence of the whole annotation might suggest the germ of a spoken word poem. The overall tenor of the annotation is open-ended and not entirely clear. It could simply be joining together SASO—an organization Biko helped establish and which has had an ongoing role in militant student politics—with an updated version of the title. It could also be a riposte to SASO, an organization with strong working-class roots whose militaristic and violent forms of protest have alienated some, especially a new black middle-class post-apartheid generation invested in "cooler" forms of politics and self-styling. The writer hence warns SASO that however authoritarian they may be, the writer will continue to express himself/herself as s/he sees fit.

The Experience of Reading, the Reading of Experience

The versions of *The Making* and *IWWIL* that I examined are all "career library books"—to use the marvelous phrase from H. J. Jackson, the scholar of marginalia—and hence presuppose an actual or aspirant community of professional and specialist readers.[25] Yet, within this community, we can detect different reading styles and modes of engagement. The readers of *The Making* were dutiful and attentive, creating their own trail of highlights and asterisks through the text. But in not one case, from the versions I have seen and with the exception of Julius Lewin, did the book move any of its university readers to use the blank space of the margins to comment or respond to the text. It is as if *The Making* is so massive, monumental, and complete that it requires no comment or leaves no room for responses. All that South African readers can do is dutifully internalize it or, like Lewin, admire, and then apply it to South Africa, rather like an imperial kit from the metropolis. By contrast, *IWWIL* turned most readers into annotators, creating writers from readers, even if only on a miniature scale.

In drawing these distinctions, it may appear that I am assigning the texts too neatly to readerly and writerly slots. In this binary scenario, *The Making* becomes like a monumental nineteenth-century realist novel that requires the reader simply to consume its fixed meaning, while *IWWIL* is open-ended, full of gaps that the reader must complete. In part this distinction has some truth, especially if we consider the ways in which both texts were produced. Based on decades of archival labor and written over three years, *The Making* is an almost moral search for epic completeness and an error-free truth, or as the epigraph to *The Poverty of Theory* says, "To leave error unrefuted is to encourage intellectual immorality."[26]

IWWIL by contrast was not conceived of as a book and instead comprises a posthumous gathering together of pamphlets, columns, speeches, trial records, and interviews that was produced hastily under conditions of savage political repression. As others have pointed out, Biko's practices of reading and writing were necessarily selective and strategic as he scanned and poached ideas from a range of writers—Fanon, Cone, Malcolm X, Senghor, Freire, Césaire.[27] Ideas were meant to be quotable, usable, and applicable, producing a model of textual practice that approximated a homemade scripturalism by which the purpose of texts was to be quoted and applied in a process that could authorize the speech of those who uttered the quotations. This practice forms part a long Christian-inflected tradition in black South African intellectual thought, where knowledge was exegetical and expository rather than empirical. Unsurprisingly, in a second-hand bookshop near the campus, it was always Biko, Fanon, and the Bible that had to be kept under lock and key.[28]

Biko's text makes a virtue of necessity: produced on the run and in bits and pieces, its incompleteness invites readers to comment, disagree, extend, and embellish. It is an experiment in which readers are asked to bring their own experience of oppression to the text and to put the two into dialogue. This mode of reading in turn formed part of a wider set of textual practices that arose in response to political repression where books were routinely banned and had to be circulated clandestinely. Rachel Matteau has documented how activists read and circulated banned books under apartheid and she shows how people seldom had the luxury of reading a whole text before it had to be passed on, hidden, or destroyed. In many cases, one never received an actual book at all; instead one got a photocopy of a section of the book.[29]

In his discussion of *IWWIL*, Premesh Lalu describes the importance and potency of the text as lying in its incompleteness. As he demonstrates, there have been numerous attempts to "complete" Biko's story: by absorbing him into histories of African nationalism and the new state; by padding out *IWWIL* into a biographical text; or by turning Biko into a prophet of reconciliation. Yet, as Lalu argues, the text insists on self-writing and on subjectivity in writing, a theme that has been obscured by these conventional histories that see the interiority of the self and the exteriority of the state as distinct domains: "Working on the self was clearly, in the ANC's view, no match for sovereign power."[30]

Such contrasts between open- and closed-ended texts obscure the similarities that exist between Biko and Thompson. Both writers work with ideas of experience, the ordinary, and the everyday as the basis for consciousness, whether this led to race or class self-awareness or some confederacy in between. Indeed, Joan Wallach Scott's critique of Thompson's class essentialism could as well be applied to Biko's ideas of race.[31] Likewise, feminist critiques of Thompson's gender normativity apply equally to Biko, for whom the black subject is always male. A further similarity would be a sense of political urgency and activism: both thinkers share a strong commitment to the future and to the possibility of changing circumstances through activism. Given this context, both writers, unsurprisingly, manifest a love of polemical and disputatious prose. As thinkers influenced by the spirit of the broader 1968 moment, they bear the imprimatur of this era in their skepticism of centralized organization and their notions of identity politics.

Given the reading formations in South Africa into which these texts were folded, these family resemblances were seldom, if ever pursued. Instead, *The Making* became drawn into a broader white radical intellectual formation whose boundary, as Ally argues, arose in part as a defensive response to BC. In her words, "the content of [the] class-based critique of apartheid was not disconnected from the characteristics of its producers—white, English-speaking intellectuals."[32]

To the social history-inclined strand of this group, *The Making* represented a usable past, or a usable model for making a past. Invested in an anti-apartheid project, this grouping focused on creating a new history for a new nation.[33] Given the emphasis on history from below, this work was almost entirely concerned with black communities and personalities. *The Making* provided a model of what a radical nation based on class should look like, how it might be narrativized, and how through careful archival labor one might represent the experience of others. *The Making* could hence "solve" the contradictory imperatives, and indeed social location, of this group: South African yet "English"; producing texts that were white-authored but were somehow "black"; were about race but were "really" about class; and being national while also being derived from the former empire.

As Robert Gregg and Madhavi Kale have argued, Thompson's work provided a portable model for those in search of constructing national labor histories in isolation whether from empire and/or race and gender. The South African reception of *The Making* provides an especially acute example of this process. The global anti-apartheid struggle created a hypernationalism that made Thompson's brand of radical patriotism useful, while the emergence of BC turned class analysis into a way of "escaping" race politics. As a text that offered a radical configuration of class and nation, *The Making* could function as a useful proxy, providing a white, English pedigree for anti-apartheid social history that its authors could not enunciate themselves.

***Isabel Hofmeyr** is Professor of African Literature at the University of the Witwatersrand and Global Distinguished Professor at New York University. She has worked extensively on the Indian Ocean world and oceanic themes more generally. Recent publications include* Gandhi's Printing Press: Experiments in Slow Reading *(2013) and a special issue of* Comparative Literature *(2016) on 'Oceanic Routes' co-edited with Kerry Bystrom. She heads up a project Oceanic Humanities for the Global South with partners from Mozambique, Mauritius, India, Jamaica and Barbados.*

Notes

1. Patricia Meyer Spacks, *On Rereading* (Cambridge, MA: Belknap Press of Harvard University Press, 2011), blurb on jacket flap.
2. "Thompson in South African Historiography," email forum established by Keith Breckenridge; and comments in response to "The Making of the English Working Class Fifty Years On," *History Workshop Online*, accessed 28 December 2014, http://www.historyworkshop.org.uk/the-making-of-the-english-working-class-fifty-years-on/.
3. "Thompson in South African Historiography."
4. Shireen Ally, "Oppositional Intellectualism as Reflection, not Rejection, of Power: Wits Sociology, 1975–1989," *Transformations* 59 (2005): 66–97; Nurina Ally and Shireen Ally, "Critical Intellectualism: The Role of Black Consciousness in Reconfiguring the Race-Class Problematic in South Africa," in *Biko Lives! Contesting the Legacies of Steve Biko*, ed. Andile Mngxitama, Amanda Alexander, and Nigel C. Gibson (London: Palgrave Macmillan, 2008), 171–188.
5. These points are based on my own memory of the period and would be common cause to anyone involved in the social history movement in South Africa.
6. "Thompson in South African Historiography"; Belinda Bozzoli and Peter Delius, eds., special edition of *Radical History Review* on "History from South Africa," 46/7 (1990).
7. Ally, "Oppositional Intellectualism"; Ally and Ally, "Critical Intellectualism."
8. Dan Magaziner, *The Law and the Prophets: Black Consciousness in South Africa, 1968–1979* (Johannesburg: Jacana, 2010).
9. Mngxitama et al., *Biko Lives!*
10. Quoted in Ally, "Oppositional Intellectualism," 73.
11. Ally, "Oppositional Intellectualism," 80 and 73.
12. These are the original 1963 Victor Gollancz edition and its subsequent impressions (like most Gollancz books it had a yellow cover, "wasp-yellow" to use the words of Nadine Gordimer, another Gollancz author); the 1968 Pelican edition and its subsequent impressions; the 1966 US Vintage/Knopf/Random House edition; the 1991 Penguin edition. Concerning the Gollancz edition, see Ruth Dudley Edwards, *Victor Gollancz: A Biography* (London: Victor Gollancz, 1987), 186, and Sheila Hodges, *Gollancz: The Story of a Publishing House, 1928–1978* (London: Victor Gollancz, 1978).
13. The JPL catalogue is not fully online, hence the visit in person. E. P. Thompson, *The Skyaos Papers* (New York: Pantheon, 1988). As SACat (the database of all South African libraries) indicates, there are no copies in any other public libraries in South Africa.

14. For a useful discussion of marginalia, see H. J. Jackson, *Marginalia: Readers Writing in Books* (New Haven, CT: Yale University Press, 2001); William H. Sherman, *Used Books: Marking Readers in Renaissance England* (Philadelphia: University of Pennsylvania Press, 2007); Elaine E. Whitaker, "A Collaboration of Readers: Categorization of the Annotations in Copies of Caxton's *Royal Book*," *Text* 7 (1994): 233–242.
15. See the string of online comments at "The Making of the English Working Class Fifty Years On," *History Workshop Online*, several of which make mention of the blue spine.
16. E. P. Thompson, *The Poverty of Theory: Or an Orrery of Errors* (London: Merlin Press, 1995); E. P. Thompson "Time, Work-Discipline and Industrial Capitalism," *Past and Present* 38 (December, 1967): 56–97.
17. These comments appear in a University of the Witwatersrand library copy of *IWWIL* (London: Heinemann, 1979) (BD 164957, 300027910), 20, 9, 72.
18. These appear in a UCT library copy of *IWWIL* (Johannesburg: Ravan, 1996) (98/2827) xv, 100.
19. Comment in Witwatersrand library copy of *IWWIL* (London: Bowerdean, 1996) (BD 388843, 302016838), 52.
20. Comments in Witwatersrand library copy of *IWWIL* (London: Heinemann, 1987) (BD 472286).
21. Comments in UCT library copies of *IWWIL* (Johannesburg: Ravan, 1996) (98/2827), 96, 91, (London: Bowerdean, 1996) (97/1490), 29, 28.
22. Copy in UCT library, (Johannesburg: Ravan, 1996) (98/2827), 48.
23. Copy in Witwatersrand library (London: Heinemann, 1979) (BD 164957, 300027910), 93.
24. Comments in Witwatersrand library copy (London: Bowerdean, 1996) (BD 388843, 302016838), contents page.
25. Jackson, *Marginalia*, 167.
26. Thompson, *Poverty*, epigraph.
27. Andile Mngxitama, Amanda Alexander and Nigel Gibson, "Biko Lives," in Mngxitama et al., *Biko Lives*, 13.
28. I am indebted to Khwezi Mkhize for this point, which comes from his experiences working in the second-hand bookshop.
29. Rachel Matteau, "The Circulation and Consumption of Banned Literature in Apartheid South Africa: Readership, Audience, Censorship with Reference to *I Write What I Like*" (MA Thesis, University of the Witwatersrand, 2005).
30. Premesh Lalu, "Incomplete Histories: Steve Biko, the Politics of Self-Writing and the Apparatus of Reading," *Current Writing* 16, no. 1 (2004): 107–126.
31. Joan Wallach Scott, "The Evidence of Experience," *Critical Inquiry* 17, no. 4 (1991): 773–797.
32. Ally, "Oppositional Intellectualism," 73.
33. The History Workshop at the University of the Witwatersrand, a hub of social history work, produced a series called, "New Nation, New History" for the newspaper *New Nation*. It subsequently appeared as a book, *New Nation, New History* (Johannesburg: New Nation and The History Workshop, 1989).

Chapter 8

Talking History

E. P. Thompson, C. L. R. James, and the Afterlives of Internationalism

Utathya Chattopadhyaya

Africa, O Africa, I see. Be Free ... What do I find?
Millions of Black bodies left behind
—Spartacus R, "Africa I See" (*Talking History*)

Disinterested London dived
Back into the swim of business
Or into taverns for an early beer.
"You black bastard," he heard,
And the weather reinforced the words.
—H. O. Nazareth, "Arrival"

E. P. Thompson, Beyond *The Making*

Edward Palmer Thompson rarely spoke of *The Making of the English Working Class* as a work of professional history. In an interview with Mike Merrill in 1976, while visiting New York, he said, "it was not a book written for the academic public."[1] In his words, it was a work written for the audience of the Left, the audience of working peoples he had found during his tenure as an adult education tutor through the 1950s. Suspecting that his "rather irreverent attitudes towards academic proprieties" were what made the book attractive to many professional historians, he chose to maintain critical distance from a discipline that was dominated by conservatives all over England. Instead, he sought the intellectual comradeship of other activists, claiming that the "formal and informal exchange with fellow socialists" in the Communist Party Historians Group had been the most significant aspect of his own historical practice.[2] Scholarship, for him, grew out of dialogue in groups where criticism was free and where history and theory were central subjects of discussion, not educational traditions steeped in rank conservatism. *The Making,* as a richly layered text, in other words, was forged out of dialogic relationships Thompson immersed himself in, both with working peoples and labor activists, as well as fellow Marxist scholars outside of strictly academic spaces.

In 1983, twenty years after the publication of *The Making,* amid a post-Falklands Thatcherist discourse and a somber intellectual climate, E. P. Thompson sat down to talk about the world with C. L. R. James for a film called *Talking History.*[3] As a cultural artifact, the film is a revealing testimony of the moods and sentiments of the Cold War era in England. Textually, however, it was an exercise in a kind of internationalist dialogue that had emerged in the interwar years and slowly vanished as the twentieth century came to a close. The film's historiographical significance lies in its provocative intertextuality, where the conversation between James and Thompson is rendered into several different frames of meaning by the newspaper clippings, images, video clips, and music used in the film. H. O. Nazareth's design and his patchwork of newspaper clippings, coupled with Spartacus R's Black Rock-influenced soundtrack that accompanies the videos and images—all transform the film into a heterogeneous canvas with multiple authorial functions that take the film far beyond the boundaries of the staged conversation itself.

If *The Making* was forged within Thompson's dialogue with working peoples, *Talking History* was produced within his intercourse with radically altered discourses and politics in 1980s Britain. Decolonization movements in the former British colonies in Africa and anti-racism movements in Britain had challenged the historical insularities of the white working class and its primary intellectuals. Thompson had been familiar with anti-imperialist politics since his childhood, but coloniality, whether economic or cultural, and the empire itself had not entered his scholarship.[4] By the end of the

1960s, and during his research on the "government of the forest" for what became *Whigs and Hunters*, he had delved deeper back into the eighteenth century to probe and revise the historical knowledge of law and constitutionalism in England.[5] Confronting the simultaneity of the slave trade and the Black Act led Thompson to consider the empire more substantially than he had before. In 1976, he noted how the historical profession was heavily staffed with believers in Anglo-Saxon civilizational superiority. "But if you are now living on a post-imperial island," by which he meant an England where the previously colonized are increasingly demanding a greater presence in the world as well as history writ large, he asked, "you are going to turn around and ask what does this peculiar culture of Anglo-Saxon eighteenth-century constitutionalism mean?" He added, "Wasn't it in fact more important that England was engaged deeply in the slave trade? That the East India Company was amassing its fortune and extending its territory in India? Aren't these the important things for the world to know about England, not whether the English had particular constitutional rituals?"[6] In other words, coloniality, if not the empire in a fuller sense, had finally begun to force its way into Thompson's thought, especially at a time when anti-colonialism became the primary idiom of left-wing internationalism across the world.

Talking History marks, in more animated and concrete ways than most of Thompson's writings in the 1970s and 1980s, his confrontation with questions of coloniality and his practice of internationalism. Internationalism, as political practice, has always been entwined in a tense struggle with practices of nationalism. Perry Anderson has previously argued that internationalism was an identifiable form of labor politics until World War II, after which it became hostage to discourses of capitalism and Western liberal democracy. Stalin's policy of "socialism in one country," Anderson points out, turned Lenin's internationalism into Soviet hegemony in a world of states, before American foreign policy turned internationalism into a shorthand for its imperialist foreign policy, wherein its constitutive "other" was "isolationism."[7] Welded both dialectically and dialogically, the relationship between nationalism and internationalism has been equally complementary and antagonistic, besides being fundamentally (re)shaped by histories of revolutionary labor and feminist politics.[8] Following Lenin and the Second International, the interwar period had transformed internationalism into a method of critiquing imperialism by not just upholding the right to self-determination of "nations," but also actively engaging in practices of dialogue, intellectual exchange, subversion, coordination, and political resolution between itinerant and heterogeneous voices belonging to often incongruous "nations" and "homes."[9] Internationalism was at once about creating forums where politicians, activists, and intellectuals could meet, as much as it was a way of uniting the sentiments of international conviviality in the decolonizing world. However, by the 1950s, this framework was transformed, from one about international dialogue into one that limited itself to interstate negotiations between members of states, thus undermining the original spirit of interwar internationalism.[10] When James and Thompson staged their discussion for the film in 1983, they resituated the spirit of *marxisant* internationalism that was deeply skeptical of the promises of statist and hegemonic politics, irrespective of whether it was socialist or not. Such a political posture came with its own range of blind spots, as is revealed repeatedly during the course of the film, but its presence nonetheless reinforced the afterlife of internationalism, especially as a practice whose intellectual surcharge is far from being exhausted. *Talking History* is at once an exposition of the tensions of internationalism as much as it is a re-espousal of the desire for a renewed internationalist spirit in the times of neoconservative globalization.

Internationalist Biographies, Internationalist Afterlives

C. L. R. James had not met Thompson before June 1967, when both came to attend a conference on "Workers' Control and Industrial Democracy" in Coventry. Thompson, present there to read out the *New Left Review*'s May Day Manifesto, written collaboratively by Stuart Hall, Raymond Williams, and himself, took the stage as planned. He vehemently castigated the then Labour prime minister Harold Wilson for kowtowing before capital and disciplining workers using state forces. Wilson had, by then, barely struggled through the massive currency crisis he had inherited and was already facing a series of worker strikes against the hardships caused by domestic inflationary pressures.[11]

Following Thompson's presentation, James rose to ask a question. "I have been very much interested in what this speaker had to say but I do regret very much that the author of the Manifesto, Mr. E. P. Thompson, was unable to be here himself. I think that he's one of the most remarkable figures in British politics and political theory today, but I wish to speak my mind about the Manifesto." Barely noticing the quizzical looks around the room, James continued, "The speaker says that they were disappointed in the Wilson government ... To say you are disappointed is to say you had expectations in the first place ... To be disappointed in it means you have come to have illusions."[12] After proceeding to laud the working classes of the "advanced capitalist countries" as bearers of the "future of socialism," James criticized the nationalist bias in Thompson's statement, which treated the problems of the Third World as distant and external to those of the British proletariat: a repetition, to James's mind, of past mistakes of the British Left. He said, "In my opinion, that is entirely wrong. We should agree that those who aim today at an *integration*, a necessary *integration* in the development of the Third World and the unity of the international proletariat of which Britain is a part, and a document which ... only gives a *paragraph* to the Third World is in my opinion doing what has been done in the past, and what the present situation does not require at all."[13]

Laughter surrounded James momentarily before the chair of the session calmly pointed out that the "comrade" seated next to him was, "in fact, E. P. Thompson." Thompson's response was equally measured. "Comrades. I have four things to say, and the first is this. When one looks back over the last twenty years to those men who are most far sighted, who first began to tease out the muddle of ideology in our times, who were at the same time Marxist with a hard theoretical basis, and close students of society, humanists with a tremendous response to and understanding of human culture, Comrade James is one of the first one thinks of. We owe a great deal to men like Comrade James and his work particularly."[14] While this set in motion a continuing dialogue between the two intellectuals, it is unknown whether Thompson did indeed answer why the Third World found only a sole paragraph in his 1967 May Day Manifesto.

Over the course of the fifty-two minute film in 1983, James and Thompson continued in the spirit of their first encounter. James had recently returned to England after two decades of travelling, teaching, and reporting on Caribbean and American political culture. He was, by then, renowned for his writings on Pan-Africanism in light of the Ghanaian anticolonial struggle, as well as his journalistic reportage on cricket, and books like *The Black Jacobins* (1938) and *Beyond a Boundary* (1963) had found an avid readership in England and beyond.[15] In what was to be the last decade of his life, he had become an active part of the Black community in Brixton, and met Nazareth there. Nazareth, known commonly as Naz, had previously worked for *The Leveller*, a radical Left magazine, and went on to start Penumbra Productions in 1981.[16] He recorded six lectures James gave on a tour across England, which were screened on Channel 4, and interviewed him for the *New Statesman* (1 July 1983), before asking him and Thompson to collaborate for *Talking History*.

Nazareth was witness to a rapidly changing Britain in the early 1980s. Margaret Thatcher had been in power since 1979 and the attack on worker unions, the miners' strike, and the increasing unemployment massively transformed the nature of British public discourse.[17] While Thatcherism was taking its own course, the landscape of television and film also changed profoundly.[18] With funding from the British Film Institute in 1975, Horace Ove had directed the first full feature by a Black British filmmaker, titled *Pressure*, which provided the momentum for greater representation of non-white themes.[19] Channel 4 capitalized on this momentum once it started operations in 1982, and its subsequent patronage of "ethnic" media created a highly popular space for various Black and Asian diasporic filmmakers.[20] As the genre of the British telefilm with its diasporic and postcolonial content emerged, Channel 4 funded several film workshops through the 1980s, which led to the formation of the Association of Black Workshops, before finally facing a deep crunch in finances by 1991. Nazareth had worked with Ove and others on *The Garland* (1981) before Ove made *Playing Away* (1986), a film about a cricket match between Brixton XI and a white "traditional

English village team." In the 1970s, Nazareth was also active, with other British Asians such as Farrukh Dhondy—in 1987, the two collaborated for the Writers Talk series at the Institute for Contemporary Arts, Mala Sen, and Vivan Sundaram in the British Black Panther Movement.[21] Nazareth later produced *Suffer the Children* (1988) on the abuse of South African children under apartheid and *Doctors and Torture* (1990) on the complicity of the medical establishment in torture practices in Latin America. His penchant for history and historians led him to Eqbal Ahmed, with whom he made *Stories My Country Told Me* (1996), one in a film series with Eric Hobsbawm, Desmond Tutu, and others discussing the relationship between culture and nationalism in their own specific contexts.

For *Talking History*, Nazareth had approached the International Defence and Aid Fund in London, which generously supported the film. By 1980, the fund had established several branches worldwide in its campaign to provide legal and financial relief to victims of apartheid rule in South Africa.[22] The fund included many members of the Conservative Party, such as Peter Bottomley, member of Parliament under Margaret Thatcher, who was invited by Fred Halliday after he left the editorial board of the *New Left Review*, to speak alongside Joan Ruddock, the then chairperson of the Campaign for Nuclear Disarmament, on 7 February 1984, when the film was screened at the Institute for Contemporary Arts in London.[23] At the event, Bottomley spoke highly of James's optimism regarding formal decolonization efforts in Africa and South America, although the interests behind Bottomley's endorsements were a different matter. More importantly, this complex biography of *Talking History* reveals the messiness of political and creative umbrella alliances that Nazareth had to navigate, amidst the throes of anti-imperial decolonization and the postwar arms race.

Nazareth began working on *Talking History* in 1983, the year that saw the publication of three path-breaking critiques of nationalism and "tradition."[24] Outside academic history, socialist internationalists came face to face with other stark realities. Blasts from the test sites of nuclear bombs resonated across Eastern Kazakhstan, Nevada, and the Pacific Islands, while pacifist protesters and the "Greenham women" marched on April Fool's Day to form a fourteen mile-long human chain connecting the Aldermaston nuclear facility with a weapons factory and a proposed missile base, to bring attention to the expanding shadow of militarization in England.[25] *Solidarity* succeeded in forcing the retreat of martial law in Poland and Lech Walesa won the Nobel Peace Prize. A massive outflux of Ghanaian refugees from Nigeria preceded the Nigerian democratic elections (a military coup followed late in the year), and the Internet as we know it today was formally launched. By the end of 1983, revolutionary politics was front and center in the world—the first xenophobic anti-Tamil riots in Sri Lanka led to the congealing of the Tamil liberation movement in Sri Lanka and among the Tamil diaspora in Britain and Canada; the Zapatista Army of National Liberation was founded in the Chiapas; the Palestine Liberation Organization remained at war on several fronts; military rule was forced to end in Argentina in December; and the news of bombings by the Irish Republican Army littered the headlines.

Against this tempestuous background, it was *Solidarity* in Poland and the peace movement in Europe that kept James and Thompson the most preoccupied. Although both of them acknowledged the global dimensions of the Cold War and the internationalist movements that opposed it, their gaze only fleetingly shifted away from Europe. The film captures both Thompson's rightful skepticism and James's hopeful optimism about *Solidarity,* since both agreed that it was of "historic importance." *Solidarity* was a breath of fresh air to the antibloc mobilization in Europe since the early 1970s, occurring as it did in the backyard of the Soviet bloc out of a mass movement of independent farmers and working class trade unions. Thompson, hardly a critic of English-ness, however maintained critical distance from the inherent nationalism of *Solidarity,* and the relationship it had to the Catholic Church. The ills of nationalism, it seemed, were more apparent in Eastern Europe than in England. Whether *Solidarity* was "a little bit male chauvinist" also bothered Thompson, who posed this question to James, pointing out the conspicuous absence of women in the leadership of the movement. James's response was more optimistic, as he replied, "I know. But they have a woman that said she has told them so." The image of Anny Walentynowicz, whose dismissal for being a member of an underground trade union sparked the spread of *Solidarity,* speaking to a crowd interrupts their conversation in the film before Thompson persevered with his skepticism of the national, "But it is *still very* Polish."[26] Ironically, the working class in *The Making,* never appeared to Thompson as *"still very* English."

James's optimism about *Solidarity* was rooted in his opposition to what he termed the "bureaucratic caste," a structure of rigid disciplining officials and apparatuses that had calcified within social democratic parties and "murdered the revolution."[27] *Solidarity*'s mass appeal and rapid spread met with James's expectations as well as his enthusiasm toward anti-Stalinist articulations within the Soviet bloc.[28] Being a distant observer, he might have been unaware of such questions as to whether Solidarity was receiving funds liberally from the United States and the CIA or how it consented to or how it consented to Poland's membership in the International Monetary Fund.[29] Nonetheless, his optimism was boundless, as he went on to add, "I can't help but think that in 1968, there was an embryonic *Solidarity* in France." If James's rhetorical use of a Polish resistance movement as the yardstick for French radical movements in 1968 wasn't challenging enough to those given to thinking of Europe in conventional East-West terms, the film adds further provocation at this point by panning onto a shot of the famous graffiti on a Parisian bridge with the incomplete slogan *Realistes Demandez L'impossible* (Be realistic. Ask the impossible).

The integrated and situated simultaneity of socialist politics in the world that shaped James's internationalism on his first encounter with Thompson, is also evident in the film. In response to Thompson's question of whether the anti-imperialist struggles in the Third World are helped at all by the peace movement in the West, James vehemently suggested that the masses of people in the Third World will respond most favorably to the anti–Cold War mobilizations in the West. He cites the example of Portugal, where the military coup, following the outbreak of massive protests against Marcelo Caetano in April 1974, was a move forward in the formal decolonization of the Portuguese colonies of Angola, Mozambique, and Guineau-Bissau. To any serious movement in the "masses of the advanced countries," James contended, "there will be tremendous response from the colonial peoples." The footage in the film shows marching youth in the streets of Lisbon followed by the flags of the People's Movement for the Liberation of Angola (MPLA). Here, James's silence on the role of guerrilla warfare by the MPLA, along with the National Union for the Total Independence of Angola (UNITA) and the National Liberation Front of Angola (FNLA), besides similar movements led by the African Party for the Independence of Guinea and Cape Verde (PAIGC) and the Mozambique Liberation Front (FRELIMO), is deafening, but equally telling of the skepticism James harbored towards revolutionary nationalisms, and the elite among the colonized which took state power after formal decolonization, as well as his growing belief in pacifist mass mobilization towards the end of his life.

Thompson's investment in international pacifism against the Cold War arms race is equally revealing in the film. "A people's détente," he remarks, is the ongoing challenge to decades of rigid Cold War structures. In stark contrast to his skepticism of *Solidarity,* his hope toward the peace movement puts in perspective the "limited war" he saw being played out in the Third World and the dystopia he saw Europe turning into. Nuclear war would ruin Europe, "destroy the infrastructure of civilization," and "civilization would have to come back from the Southern hemisphere." Whether Thompson was overemphasizing the peace movement's successes or not was a valid question. When the film was screened at the Institute for Contemporary Arts, Joan Ruddock, chairperson of the Campaign for Nuclear Disarmament (CND) before resigning in 1985, noted the failure of the CND to mobilize against the Falklands War massacres, despite having overwhelming opposition to the war effort among its ranks.[30] The "Atlanticist bargain," a subservient Europe in alliance with a hegemonic muscular United States—an alliance that Thompson thought would break apart, Ruddock noted, was in fact, alive and well in 1984.

The fascinating, and often speculative, observations by Thompson and James in the film are flavored and enriched by Spartacus R's music. He shapes much of the film's internationalist biography by imbricating it in the Pan-Africanist milieu that James represented. When Nazareth asked Spartacus R to compose the score for the film, he had been bassist for Osibisa, a Black Rock band hugely popular in London in the 1960s and early 1970s. However, declining incomes in a "recession-bound Britain" led him to start his own label, Zara, a decision that coincided with his renewed search for the "acoustic kernel" of African and Caribbean string music, which could produce "a new Third World fusion."[31] His decision to go solo and shift from electronic sounds to acoustic ones meant that Nazareth could draw in a relatively raw and new Spartacus, with just the right lingering influence of rock music. "I Am the Song of Unity," which opens the film, is an obvious example of this moment where an acoustic guitar subtly undergirds his words, proving why his music was once described by the *Black Music and Jazz Review* as a combination of "furiously hot messages" and "caressing sounds."[32] The refrain in the song continues with "I am the song of love ... I am the song of liberty ... I am the Freedom Song," accompanying the images of the accused in the Treason Trial in 1956 in South Africa and the image of Hector Peterson's bloody corpse, the first casualty in the students' movement in Soweto. The images and music in the track help reinforce the dialogue between Black diasporic internationalism and African anticolonial struggles on the ground, a conversation that James was intimately a part of but did not discuss at much length in his conversation with Thompson.

Spartacus's internationalism was shaped deeply by his travels outside Europe, recording *Africa I See* across Fiji, Australia, the Caribbean, and London on a solo tour. The album combined the elements of African music across multiple sites into compositions of fiery poetry against white racism and colonial histories. For the film, Spartacus translated some of those influences into composing "Third World War," a fuller song that follows smaller musical sections that accompany the discussion on World Wars I and II. As if naming out loud to memorialize, celebrate as well as mourn, the track contains a recurrent listing of the names of decolonizing nations in the background: Algeria, Argentina, Bangladesh, India, Guatemala, and so on, enveloping the refrain "The Third World War has been raging, ever since the Second World War." "They ideologize some brothers, mili-terrorize some others, partition the religions ... so the Third World War go on forever" accompanies the stills from the Vietnam War, where children stand around with masked faces to prevent breathing in the poisonous fumes of Agent Orange. As Vietnamese women guerrillas load artillery to fire, the words "If you're living in the third world, you're living in a state of war. If you're living in the third world, you're dying in a state of war" express the narrow premium on life under imperialist occupation in most of the Cold War world.

Although *Talking History* captures Spartacus in the early stages of his attempt to produce a "Third World fusion," the influence of Black Rock remained evident in the film. Spartacus's influence was rooted in the constellation of events and discourses around Afro-Caribbean self-identification, the politics of urban riots, and the radical politics of culture among minorities in Britain.[33] The milieu is palpable in the soundtrack when the talking heads discuss Margaret Thatcher and Ronald Reagan. In "I Don't Wanna Go to War," Spartacus bares a ruthless disgust for both figures, calling Margaret "the old witch with a hatchet ... [who] wanted to send me away to clean up her shit ... somewhere out there in the Atlantic" and Reagan, "Ronnie, the rabid mercenary." The lines on Thatcher accompany the stills from Ireland and Kenya in the film, and the lines on Reagan animate the images from the American proxy war with the Sandinistas in Nicaragua. The thrice-emphasized refrain, "I told her/him once, I told her/him twice, I told her/him a thousand times. I don't wanna go to war" is at once his denunciation of war against marginalized peoples across the world and the use of Black youth as cannon fodder in the service of imperialist and nationalist objectives. Through such fighting words, which pervade all the tracks in the film, one hears the pacifist in Spartacus in a way that is deeply self-aware of the universalism of Black internationalism while being substantially rooted in the situational realities of Black life in Britain. It is this self-awareness that also marks his in-between-ness in the film, especially in relation to the acoustic sounds, which symbolized Pan-African and Black internationalist meaning for him, and the electric sounds of Black Rock music in 1970s London.

Socialist humanism meets Pan-Africanism, is how the historian Peter Linebaugh characterized the James-Thompson dialogue well before the film was made.[34] Little did he know that it would be Spartacus's presence when the dialogue was finally staged, that would materialize the spirit of Pan-Africanism for the film's audience. *Talking History* is marked by the ways in which Spartacus's musical production engages in the textual layers of the film. Spartacus's own intellectual biography was deeply shaped by traveling between sites connected with the history of slavery. His indulgence in Caribbean acoustics and his belief in global African-ness informed his music throughout his life. In the film, however, Spartacus appears to follow the agenda set by the course of the discussion between Thompson and James. Yet, in discreet moments, his music opens up dichotomies that the conversation does not address. Race and racism, of which the conversation between James and Thompson barely scratches the surface, is placed front and center by Spartacus's lyrics. The dialogue places the struggles of the African urban poor and working classes in different nationalist movements implicitly also as a struggle of racialized peoples against imperialist racist formations, but Spartacus emphasizes how the neoliberal militarism of the Reagan and Thatcher governments liberally recruited soldiers from racialized minorities to serve in overseas wars. He takes the critique from intellectual reasoning to defiant and confrontational poetry, adding texture where little was to be found. The "me" Spartacus refers to stands in for the trope of the young Black male, recruited by an imperial state to be reshaped into a loyal employee. That such nationalist co-option requires resistance across borders, both in the United States and the UK, reveals Spartacus's own investments in twentieth-century Black internationalism.

Encountering these entangled histories through the film in the 2013 symposium on Thompson's *The Making* seemed apt: besides the fiftieth anniversary of the publication of *The Making*, it was also the fiftieth anniversary of the publication of James's *Beyond a Boundary* and the seventy-fifth of the publication of *Black Jacobins*. In the thirty years following the release of the film, enormous transitions in electronic media, digital technology, and increasing corporate globalization have attempted to place several smokescreens between the anti-imperial discourses of the mid-twentieth century and the priorities of present social movements. That perceived distance is contested and often erased in the interface between the intertextual work of the film and its contemporary audience. The graphic images from the Korean War, Vietnam, and Latin America that litter the film and Spartacus R's music interspersed between issues that James and Thompson talk about, produce a genealogical effect whereby one gets a measure of how the critical legacies of twentieth-century anti-imperialism are inherited in the globalized present. Coloniality is placed at the heart of the conditions of any critical internationalist dialogue, then as well as now.

The afterlives resuscitated in the film, especially through the confrontation with the graphic life of the Cold War and the use of newspaper headlines as signposts of a rapidly changing geopolitical order, bear the capacity to provoke the viewer to historicize his or her own predilections. They open up room to critique the hopefulness as well as the pessimism of the late Cold War years that James and Thompson discuss, by drawing the audience into the conversation first hand. Afterlives, as a concept, has been recently invoked to designate the recurrence, and the incompleteness, of the past and used analytically to underscore efforts to renew, rediscover, and rethink subjective predicaments.[35] Its fluid existence within terrains of critical nostalgia, commemorative politics, and the battles over the uses of the past in Walter Benjamin's "time of the now," offers the critical historian a place for interpreting the past while enabling critiques of the present through histories which have yet to exhaust their radical surcharges.[36] The history of internationalism, specifically of revolutionary and Marxian persuasions, is enormously relevant in that regard. The interwar period was a window, or a "moment," within which internationalism proliferated through marginal yet significantly mobile bodies—lascars, seafarers, anticolonial revolutionaries, as well as public intellectuals.[37] While the revolutionary Marxist underpinnings of internationalism were most popular, other variants were also circulating wherein political self-fashioning did not imply complete theoretical clarity or rigidity. Negotiation, friction, and collaboration shaped the collision between Pan-Islamism after the fall of the Ottoman Empire, and various kinds of anticolonial revolutionary or nationalist sentiments, and even shades of fascism, in the internationalisms of the interwar period.[38] In other words, the conditions, predicaments, constraints, and excesses produced by colonial power, and the transgressions against it, were the crucible within which internationalism found its most complex and dissenting sensibilities. Such legacies of that interwar moment took distinct shapes repeatedly through the latter half of the twentieth century, of which *Talking*

History is ample evidence, especially given the interwoven histories of travel, reportage, political alliances, and funding that shaped the film and the lives of its different authors.

The anticolonial internationalism of the interwar years is an incomplete disposition, still wanting in multi-sited critique, empathy, and careful re-affirmation. If *Talking History* materializes the spirit of the interwar years, then it also resurrects this incompleteness on several counts. First, by the 1980s, besides Pan-Africanism and anti-Stalinist brands of left wing political activity, the women's movement, Maoist agrarian revolutionary politics, resource-based struggles, and rights-based social justice movements had transformed the face of internationalist activism across the world. As in the case of armed revolutionary anti-colonial and internationalist movements in Africa, which James was aware of but did not discuss, several other social movements frame the film's dialogue by making their presence felt outside the boundaries of the dialogue itself. James and Thompson, in addition to Nazareth and Spartacus, resemble only a fraction of such an effluence of internationalist political assertions in the late twentieth century, thus forcing us to ask what else we need to know in order to better understand the transformations in critical internationalism beyond the interwar years.

Second, opportunities for multidimensional self-criticism as central to the practice of internationalism, especially in the imperial metropolitan public sphere, have often been lost or unfulfilled. When Thompson tells James of how "in Britain, we've had a quiet kind of history, because we've always exported violence," his attention to British aggression overseas occludes the experiences of Irish, Afro-Caribbean, Indian, and indigenous colonial subjects who had historically made their way into the metropole, found shelter, and often rebelled against the violence of the imperial state "at home."[39] Even though Thompson sees the empire, he only sees it at a distance, elsewhere and far away, as opposed to its violent existence within Britain itself, something which Spartacus's music makes completely conspicuous.

Third, the desire to find, in revolutionary impulses elsewhere, the redemptive solace to compensate for the lack of revolutionary progress closer home, especially for the Left in the United States and Western Europe, has flattened many productive tensions and possible points of internationalist solidarity. In response to Thompson's lament of the "loss of democratic and anti-statist autonomous people's content" due to "militarization of Marxism under the influence of Post-Stalinist Soviet Union," James fervently points to "Iran, Poland, and others," including India. James finds in these sites "a socialism that is coming," where the Iranian Revolution is compared—in flat and uncritical terms—with the French Revolution. About India, Thompson notes a "gentle and anti-acquisitive popular tradition" where "it is possible not to get into the dreadful bureaucratic growth programming afflicting the rest of the world," an observation that sits quite uneasily with the history of Nehruvian developmentalism and the Green Revolution.

Nonetheless, the critical spirit of internationalism from the vantage point of the imperial metropole, however, is more palpable as the film draws to a close. Thompson reflects on the problems with "doing" history while being committed to the labor movement, especially when labor has itself been complicit in the British colonial project. "In history, one is giving back to people the history historians have confiscated from them," says Thompson about the politics of history writing, "but at the same time, the historian belongs to a discipline and one must not allow one's history to become propaganda." He goes on to list the uses of history for "terrible manipulations of public consciousness" in the case of "not only Nazism and fascism but the entire record of complicity with imperialism within western labor movements and social democratic movements." An unrelenting advocate of rigor and objectivity, especially with comrades, Thompson says, "To the Left, sometimes, one has to say—the pursuit of truth is also our business."

Furthermore, his antagonism with statist forms of politics deeply informed Thompson's internationalism. "Military organizations have become states within states"—a phrase eerily resonant with contemporary ideas of the military-industrial complex as the ersatz modern state. The slippage into interstatism within formal decolonization movements and their supporters overseas also worried Thompson. "Aid is the export of foul machines of war, military aerodromes, and military infrastructure," he remarked, such that the "Cold War, which is really the hot war in the underdeveloped world, is about arms exports." Putting a measured drag on the optimism of James toward the growing formal decolonization struggles, Thompson resituates the specter of the arms race into the discourse of emerging independent states, thus warning us against the slippage of the meanings of internationalism from dialogues between "nations" to negotiations and bargains between states. His critique of state socialism allows him to simultaneously criticize the uses of communism as a bogey. On the use of "Cold War ideology as a means of internal regulation" in the West, he says, "anti-Communism in the US is necessary even if the Soviet Union didn't exist" in order to control American radical and dissident groups and "denounce all the authentic movements of the American people as pro-commie." Throughout the film, this empathy for "authentic" democratic mass movements, coupled with a critical distance from state interventions, hold up the internationalist spirit of Thompson's approach, gradually unsettling the viewer even as it cautiously reassures them.

E. P. Thompson, Beyond *Talking History*

So where does *Talking History* leave us, as members of reading publics, engaging with Thompson's legacy fifty years since the publication of his magnum opus? The film, as I have argued, is a textual product bound with the complex history of critical internationalism. It is deeply shaped by the practices of travel, radical forms of political solidarity, constantly transforming intellectual culture, and universalist dispositions that are never shorn of their situated particularisms. The film also has multiple authors, who take its textual power to diverse ends. It enframes the encounter between two Marxist internationalist intellectuals, both historians with a love for epic narratives, at a time when such forms of dialogue were vanishing. It also records Thompson's engagement with coloniality in ways that his other writings do not; here, he is not bound by the academic proprieties he so detested when he wrote *The Making*. In the hands of Nazareth and Spartacus, the film's textures transform in their affective capacities and dissident aesthetics. Spartacus presents the voice of an assertive colonized "Other" within Britain, at a time when neoliberalism was gradually being conjoined with British belligerence in other parts of the world. All of these factors make *Talking History* a challenging addendum to one's engagement with *The Making*, especially since the film, much like the book, was not intended for the purely academic public. The finer points of Thompson's critique, whether of statism or the complicity of European social democratic movements in imperial projects, casts his ways of thinking about the world into sharp relief. Understanding his rhetorical and analytical approach within the enormous textual breadth as well as discursive limitations of both the book and the film, enables us to understand Thompson in a much fuller sense, and contextualize his intellectual trajectory both within and without disciplinary history.

However, the sense of incompleteness that marks the film is also a call for us to rethink where the spirit of interwar internationalism can be resuscitated in the critique of nation-states. From our own historical vantage point, there are several possible conversations around globalization and nation-states, which the discussion between Thompson and James prefigured, but did not exhaust. Where the dialogue between James and Thompson reveals some of the inadequacies of their way of viewing post war Europe and the Cold War world, it also invites the discerning viewer to go, in James's words, "below, because it is below that you can make your history contemporary." It is in that spirit, that one hopes to proceed.

Utathya Chattopadhyaya *is Assistant Professor of History at the University of California, Santa Barbara. He teaches and writes about histories of capital, commodities, and labor in colonial South Asia, the British Empire, and the Indian Ocean World.*

Notes

I thank Antoinette Burton for her detailed comments and arguments over several drafts of this article. Thanks also to Linda Mitchell and Daniel Gordon for their feedback and editorial assistance. David Roediger provided perceptive feedback on the final draft and James Barrett was unfailingly encouraging. Madhavi Kale's questions at the end of the film screening provoked some of the thoughts presented above. I also thank Zachary Poppel who co-organized the screening and publicity of *Talking History* with me.

1. Mike Merrill, "Interview with E. P. Thompson," in *Visions of History,* ed. H. Abelove, B. Blackmar, P. Dimock, J. Schneer (New York: Pantheon Books, 1983), 7. The interview is one among similar ones with other radical historians, all conducted by the Mid-Atlantic Radical Historians' Organization.
2. *Visions of History,* 13. Dona Torr's presence was crucial in the Communist Party Historians Group. For a summary of her influence on Thompson's work, see David Renton, *Dissident Marxism: Past Voices for Present Times* (London: Zed Books, 2004), 104–120.
3. *Talking History,* Penumbra Productions (52 min), London, 1983. Directed by H. O. Nazareth and financed by Greater London Council for Funding Aid and the International Defence and Aid Fund, the film was distributed internationally by Other Cinema Ltd. For an archived list of Penumbra films, see the British Film Institute archive, accessed 10 October 2014, http://explore.bfi.org.uk/4ce2b94fdb349.
4. Thompson's father, a liberal Englishman close to Nehru, Tagore, and others, shaped much of Thompson's childhood. The only glimpse of coloniality in *The Making* surrounds Thompson's minor discussion of the Irish. Race and gender are absent, either as identities or as categories of analysis, in *The Making.* For selective criticisms and revisions, see Carolyn Steedman, *Master and Servant: Love and Labour in the English Industrial Age* (Cambridge: Cambridge University Press, 2007); Catherine Hall, *The Tale of Samuel and Jemima: Gender and Working Class Culture in Nineteenth-Century England,* in *E. P. Thompson: Critical Perspectives,* ed. H. Kaye and K. McClelland (Philadelphia: Temple University Press, 1990); Madhavi Kale and Robert Gregg, "The Empire and Mr. Thompson: Making of Indian Princes and English Working Class," *Economic and Political Weekly* 32, no. 36 (1997): 2273–2288.
5. E. P. Thompson, *Whigs and Hunters: The Origin of the Black Act* (London: Allen Lane, 1975).
6. Abelove et al., *Visions of History,* 9.
7. Unfortunately, this useful, albeit Eurocentric, periodization appears only as an editorial in the *New Left Review.* See Perry Anderson, "Internationalism: A Breviary," *New Left Review* 14 (2002): 5–25. For an explication of Anderson's longer engagement with internationalism, see George Eliot, *Perry Anderson: The Merciless Laboratory of History* (Minneapolis: University of Minnesota Press, 1998), 130–133.
8. A fuller treatment of such histories of internationalism is beyond the scope of this article. For a preliminary volume on communist internationalism, see Marcel van der Linden and Frits van Holthoon, eds., *Internationalism in the Labour Movement, 1830–1940* (Leiden: Brill, 1988). For a recent study of black internationalism in the imperial metropole, see Marc Matera, "Black Internationalism and African and Caribbean Intellectuals in London, 1919–1950" (PhD diss., Rutgers University, 2008). For an appraisal of avowedly liberal forms of internationalism

that deny its revolutionary antecedents, see Glenda Sluga, *Internationalism in the Age of Nationalism* (Philadelphia: University of Pennsylvania Press, 2013).

9. Recent scholarship on internationalism within the complex fabric of the interwar years has made several such voices legible in alternative frames. See Ali Raza, Franziska Roy, and Benjamin Zachariah eds., *The Internationalist Moment: South Asia, Worlds and Worldviews 1917–1939* (New Dehli: Sage, 2014), xi–xli. Thanks are due to Benjamin Zachariah for sharing the unpublished manuscript with me.
10. With regard to Europe, Perry Anderson attributes this to a complicated set of factors, especially Stalin's policies in East Europe. See Anderson, *Internationalism.*
11. Peter Jones, *America and the British Labour Party: The Special Relationship at Work* (London: I. B. Tauris, 1997), 138.
12. Christian Hogsbjerg, "People's History and Socialist Theory: When E. P. Thompson met C. L. R. James," presented at the Historical Materialism conference, London, November 2013. This is excerpted from a larger quotation in the paper. Thanks are due to the author for sharing the unpublished paper with me. The abstract is available at http://www.historicalmaterialism.org/conferences/annual10/submit/people2019s-history-and-socialist-theory-when-e.p.-thompson-met-c.l.r.-james, accessed 19 February 2014.
13. Ibid.; emphasis added.
14. Hogsbjerg has recounted, in his ongoing research on the long relationship and correspondence between James and Thompson, different responses from the audience at the event. I am indebted to him for sharing his notes with me. See Christian Hogsbjerg, *C. L. R. James in Imperial Britain* (Durham: Duke University Press, 2014), 35–36.
15. Both works have now run into multiple editions. For the original publications, see C. L. R. James, *The Black Jacobins* (London: Purnell & Sons, 1938), and *Beyond a Boundary* (London: Stanley Paul & Co., 1963). On the relevance of *Black Jacobins* to race and class analysis in James's oeuvre, see Grant Farred, "First Stop: Port-au-Prince: Mapping Postcolonial Africa Through Toussaint L'Ouverture and His Black Jacobins," in *The Politics of Culture in the Shadow of Capital*, ed. Lisa Lowe and David Lloyd (Durham, NC: Duke University Press, 1997), 227–247.
16. Suman Bhuchar, "H. O. Nazareth," in *Companion to Contemporary Black British Culture*, ed. Alison Donnell (London: Routledge, 2002). The opening epigraph to this article is excerpted from *Arrival*. See H. O. Nazareth, *Lobo* (London and Bombay: Clearing House, Penumbra Productions, 1984), 32. *Lobo* is Nazareth's collection of autobiographical poetry re-telling his passage to England and *Arrival* captures his first few moments at Victoria Station.
17. These adverse effects upon the British welfare state are celebrated by conservative writers even now. For a recent recounting, see Graham Stewart, *Bang! A History of Britain in the 1980s* (London: Atlantic Books, 2013).
18. Thatcherism, shorthand for a neoconservative and vicious radical Right that emerged in the 1980s, was identified by Stuart Hall as an ailment to be cured with a renewed path toward socialism. He ended with the question, "Is there a doctor in the house?" See Stuart Hall, "Thatcherism: A New Stage?" *Marxism Today* (February 1980): 26–28.
19. See Sean Cubitt, "Diasporan Film-Makers," in *Encyclopedia of Contemporary British Culture*, ed. Peter Childs and Mike Storry (London: Routledge, 1999).
20. This also led to conservatives fearing that "loonies were being let on air." See Paul Giles, "History with Holes: Channel 4 Television Films of the 1980s," in

Fires Were Started: British Cinema and Thatcherism, 2nd ed., ed. Lester D. Friedman (London: Wallflower, 2006), 58–76.

21. Darcus Howe, later editor of *Race Today,* who joined the Panthers after his arrest as one of the Mangrove Nine in 1970, remembers, in quite acerbic terms, their presence in the Youth League meetings at the Oval House. See Robin E. R. Bunce and Paul Field, Darcus Howe: *A Political Biography* (London: Bloomsbury Academic, 2014), 138–139. See also Farrukh Dhondy's biographical memoir of James and his role in shaping *Freedom News,* the newsletter of the Youth League in Farrukh Dhondy, *C. L. R. James: Cricket, the Caribbean and World Revolution* (London: Weidenfeld and Nicolson, 2001).
22. Few scholars have entirely worked out the nature of secret efforts the International Defence and Aid Fund made for South African anti-colonialism. See Denis Herbstein, *White Lies: Canon Collins and the Secret War Against Apartheid* (Cape Town: HSRC Press, 2004). For a discussion of the relationship between Canon John Collins, who spearhead the IDAF, and Oliver Tambo, see Luli Callinicos, *Oliver Tambo: Beyond the Engeli Mountains* (Claremont: David Philip, 2004), 244.
23. A recording of the discussion following the screening of the film can be found in the Institute for Contemporary Arts Talks series of the British Library Sound Archive, accessed 21 March 2014, http://sounds.bl.uk/Arts-literature-and-performance/ICA-talks/024M-C0095X0092XX-0100V0.
24. See Ernest Gellner, *Nations and Nationalism* (Ithaca, NY: Cornell University Press, 1983); Benedict Anderson, *Imagined Communities: Reflections on the Origin and Spread of Nationalism* (London: Verso, 1983); and Terence Ranger and Eric Hobsbawm, eds., *The Invention of Tradition* (Cambridge: Cambridge University Press, 1983).
25. For a volume commemorating the event, see Alice Cook and Gwyn Kirk, *Greenham Women Everywhere: Dreams, Ideas, and Actions form the Women's Peace Movement* (London: Pluto Press, 1983).
26. Emphasis added.
27. James's faith in the "instinctive" participation of classes in the class struggle, which he saw with the French Revolution, was fundamental to this critique of bureaucratization, especially after he had parted ways with Trotsky. See C. L. R. James, *Notes on Dialectics: Hegel, Marx, Lenin* (Westport, CT: Lawrence Hill, 1981), 181–183, 185.
28. For a discussion of James's optimism about an anti-Stalinist socialism emerging in Europe, see Frank Rosengarten, *Urbane Revolutionary: C. L. R. James and the Struggle for a New Society* (Jackson: University Press of Mississippi, 2008), 98–100.
29. These are pressing questions with few answers, yet. See Tony Judt, *Postwar: A History of Europe since 1945* (New York: Penguin Books, 2006), 589, 606, 631.
30. Ruddock later joined the successive Labour governments of Blair and Brown before becoming Dame Ruddock. See John Bingham, "From CND Activist to Dame for Joan Ruddock," *Daily Telegraph,* 31 December 2011, accessed 22 March 2013, http://www.telegraph.co.uk/news/uknews/honours-list/8985279/New-Year-Honours-2012-From-CND-activist-to-Dame-for-Joan-Ruddock.html. Her speech is archived at the British Library Sound Archive.
31. Black Rock was self-identified as such by Afro-Caribbean British rock musicians. See Daniel Vaona, "Front Liners: Daniel Vaona Talks to Spartacus R," *Black Music and Jazz Review* 5, no.6 (October 1982): 14.
32. Ibid.

33. Stuart Hall and the work of the Race and Politics group at Birmingham still remain capacitive of illuminating this moment. See Center for Contemporary Cultural Studies, *The Empire Strikes Back: Race and Racism in 70s Britain* (London: Hutchinson, 1982). For a later argument on the possibilities of race and cultural analysis in critical forms of politics, see Paul Gilroy, *There Ain't No Black in the Union Jack* (London: Unwin Hyman, 1987).
34. Peter Linebaugh, "What if C. L. R. James Had Met E.P. Thompson in 1792?" *Urgent Tasks* no. 12 (1981), accessed 24 June 2014, http://www.sojournertruth.net/epthompson.html.
35. In the context of millenarian protest movements in the British Empire, and the Xhosa cattle killings in particular, see Jennifer Wenzel, *Bulletproof: Afterlives of Anticolonial Prophecy in South Africa and Beyond* (Chicago: University of Chicago Press, 2009).
36. Walter Benjamin's *Jetztzeit* in his *Theses on the Philosophy of History,* wherein the historian's "concept of the present" is the "time of the now," in a dialectic where time and history are constructed against the mere "continuum of history" by the positing of one "era" in a constellation against another, shapes Wenzel's argument in *Bulletproof.* See Hannah Arendt, ed., *Walter Benjamin: Illuminations* (New York: Schocken Books, 2007), 261, 263.
37. Print culture was significant to many of these changes. See Ali Raza, Franziska Roy, and Benjamin Zachariah, eds., *The Internationalist Moment: South Asia, Worlds and Worldviews 1917–39* (New Delhi: Sage, 2014). On the politics of lascars (maritime workers from the Indian colonies in the imperial naval world), see Ali Raza and Benjamin Zacharia, "To Take Arms across a Sea of Trouble: The 'Lascar System,' Politics, and Agency in the 1920's," *Itinerario* 36, no. 3 (2012): 19–38.
38. See Raza et al., *The Internationalist Moment.*
39. Several academic works in new imperial history, diaspora histories, and critiques of British multiculturalism have often pointed this out. Most recently, popular histories have also begun to address such questions. For one such example, see Clive Bloom, *Violent London: 2000 Years of Riots, Rebels, and Revolts,* rev. ed. (London: Palgrave Macmillan, 2010).

Index